T&T CLARK STUDY GUIDES TO THE OLD TESTAMENT

Jonah, Micah and Nahum

Series Editor
Adrian Curtis, University of Manchester, UK
Published in association with the Society for Old Testament Study

OTHER TITLES IN THE SERIES INCLUDE:

Amos: An Introduction and Study Guide
1 & 2 Kings: An Introduction and Study Guide
1 & 2 Samuel: An Introduction and Study Guide
Daniel: An Introduction and Study Guide
Ecclesiastes: An Introduction and Study Guide
Exodus: An Introduction and Study Guide
Ezra-Nehemiah: An Introduction and Study Guide
Genesis: An Introduction and Study Guide
Haggai, Zechariah and Malachi: An Introduction and Study Guide
Jeremiah: An Introduction and Study Guide
Job: An Introduction and Study Guide
Joel, Obadiah, Habakkuk, Zephaniah: An Introduction and Study Guide
Joshua: An Introduction and Study Guide
Leviticus: An Introduction and Study Guide
Numbers: An Introduction and Study Guide
Proverbs: An Introduction and Study Guide
Psalms: An Introduction and Study Guide
Song of Songs: An Introduction and Study Guide

T & T CLARK STUDY GUIDES TO THE NEW TESTAMENT:

1, 2, and 3 John: An Introduction and Study Guide
1 Peter: An Introduction and Study Guide
1 & 2 Thessalonians: An Introduction and Study Guide
2 Corinthians: An Introduction and Study Guide
Colossians: An Introduction and Study Guide
Ephesians: An Introduction and Study Guide
Hebrews: An Introduction and Study Guide
James: An Introduction and Study Guide
John: An Introduction and Study Guide
Luke: An Introduction and Study Guide
Mark: An Introduction and Study Guide
Matthew: An Introduction and Study Guide
Philemon: An Introduction and Study Guide
Philippians: An Introduction and Study Guide
Revelation: An Introduction and Study Guide
Romans: An Introduction and Study Guide
The Acts of the Apostles: An Introduction and Study Guide
The Letters of Jude and Second Peter: An Introduction and Study Guide

Jonah, Micah and Nahum

An Introduction and Study Guide

Julie Woods

t&tclark
LONDON • NEW YORK • OXFORD • NEW DELHI • SYDNEY

T&T CLARK

Bloomsbury Publishing Plc, 50 Bedford Square, London, WC1B 3DP, UK
Bloomsbury Publishing Inc, 1385 Broadway, New York, NY 10018, USA
Bloomsbury Publishing Ireland, 29 Earlsfort Terrace, Dublin 2, D02 AY28, Ireland

BLOOMSBURY, T&T CLARK and the T&T Clark logo are trademarks of
Bloomsbury Publishing Plc

First published in Great Britain 2025
Copyright © Julie Woods, 2025

Julie Woods has asserted her right under the Copyright, Designs and Patents Act, 1988, to be identified as Author of this work.

For legal purposes the Acknowledgements on p. x constitute an extension of this copyright page.

Cover design by clareturner.co.uk

All rights reserved. No part of this publication may be: i) reproduced or transmitted in any form, electronic or mechanical, including photocopying, recording or by means of any information storage or retrieval system without prior permission in writing from the publishers; or ii) used or reproduced in any way for the training, development or operation of artificial intelligence (AI) technologies, including generative AI technologies. The rights holders expressly reserve this publication from the text and data mining exception as per Article 4(3) of the Digital Single Market Directive (EU) 2019/790.

Bloomsbury Publishing Plc does not have any control over, or responsibility for, any third-party websites referred to or in this book. All internet addresses given in this book were correct at the time of going to press. The author and publisher regret any inconvenience caused if addresses have changed or sites have ceased to exist, but can accept no responsibility for any such changes.

A catalogue record for this book is available from the British Library.

A catalog record for this book is available from the Library of Congress.

ISBN: HB: 978-0-5676-9669-4
PB: 978-0-5676-9668-7
ePDF: 978-0-5676-9671-7
eBook: 978-0-5676-9670-0

Series: T&T Clark Study Guides to the Old Testament

Typeset by Newgen KnowledgeWorks Pvt. Ltd., Chennai, India
Printed and bound in Great Britain

To find out more about our authors and books visit www.bloomsbury.com and sign up for our newsletters.

Dedicated to Frederick Jowett with love.
Thank you for enabling me to do what I do.

Contents

Acknowledgements x
List of Abbreviations xi

1 Introduction 1

2 Jonah 3

Introduction 3
Categorizing Jonah 4
    Identifying Jonah 4
    Locating Jonah in time and space 4
    Authoring Jonah 6
Jonah's literary characteristics 7
    Genre 7
    Larger-than-life language 10
    Humour 10
    Non-factual elements 11
Structure and patterns 12
Jonah through the ages 13
Jonah 1 – rising up to go down 14
Jonah 2 – inside the he-fish-she-fish 20
Jonah 3 – an evangelist's dream, but Jonah's nightmare 26
Jonah 4 – plant, worm, wind and sun – and many
    animals 31
Concluding reflections on the book of Jonah as
    Scripture 38
References 39

3 Nahum 43

Introduction 43
Nahum and his audience 43
Setting Nahum in place and time 44
The text of Nahum 46
    Time of writing 46
    The putative broken acrostic 46
    Transmission and redaction 47
Genres 48
    OANs as oracles or burdens 48
    Visions and word 49
    The genre of acrostic poems 50
    Woe oracles 51
Nahum's poetry 51
Nahum 1 – God's nature and responsibilities 52
Nahum 2 – revenge is sweet! Or is it? 55
Nahum 3 – Nineveh broken beyond repair 57
    Shaming or rape 57
    Detested things 60
    Quotation marks and speaker 61
    No-amon and a reading strategy for Nahum 61
    Locusts and stars 63
Nahum's theological purpose 64
    Nahum's audiences 64
    Dulce et decorum est 65
    A voice for the oppressed 67
Concluding remarks: Nahum for everybody 67
References 70

4 Micah 73

Introduction 73
Historical and geographical setting 73
    Historical setting 73
    Who is Micah? 74
    Geographical setting 75
Dating 76
Translations 77
Literary artistry and structure 78

    Literary artistry 78
    Genre and form 79
    Structure and coherence 80
    Micah in the twelve 81
    Micah between Jonah and Nahum in MT 83
  Other theological purposes and themes 86
  Micah in the contemporary world 87
    Reasons for lament (Mic. 1.8-11) 87
    Punishment-town wordplays (Mic. 1.10-16) 88
    Land grabbing and identity (Mic. 2.1-2) 88
    Responsibility not reliance (Mic. 3.9-11; 6.8) 90
    Isaiah and Micah talk together (Mic. 5.9-14 and Isa.
      2.6-22) 90
    God cannot be bribed (Mic. 6.1-8) 91
    Theophanies reworked (Mic. 7.7-20) 91
    Trauma studies and Micah (Mic. 1.6-7; 4.1-5, 9-10;
      5.3) 92
    Micah in Africa (Mic. 2.12-13; 3.5; 6.6-8; 7.1-6) 93
  Conclusion 93
  References 94

Scriptural Index 99
Subject Index 105

Acknowledgements

I would like to thank all those at Bloomsbury, particularly for their patience and understanding of my health issues which were diagnosed after I had agreed to write this and which still dominate. My particular thanks go to my editor and friend, Adrian Curtis, for inviting me to write this volume and for careful reading of it, as well as his patience. I am also grateful to Walter Moberly for reading a draft of this monograph. Finally, my thanks go to Fred Jowett and Tim Price for the practical help they have given me, such as doing the shopping or making the evening meal when I've been working late. Fred has been there since before the start of my formal theological education and I dedicate this work to him.

Abbreviations

ANE	Ancient Near East
AV	Authorized Version (also known as KJV)
ESV	English Standard Version
ET	English Translation
GNB	Good News Bible (also called Good News Translation (GNT))
JPS	Jewish Publication Society
KJV	King James' Version (also known as AV)
LXX	Septuagint
MT	Masoretic Text
NASB	New American Standard Bible
NEB	New English Bible
NIV	New International Version
NJB	New Jerusalem Bible
NRSV	New Revised Standard Version
NE	Northeast
NT	New Testament
OANs	Oracles against the nations
OT	Old Testament
PhD	Doctor of Philosophy

Syr	Syriac (version)
TANAK	What Jewish people sometimes call the OT (OT being a Christian term)
Tg	Targum
Vg	Vulgate

1

Introduction

Jonah, Micah and Nahum occur in that order in the MT. Given that so many people advise reading Jonah and Nahum together because of their common focus on Nineveh, I will deal with Nahum after Jonah. Finally, I will look at Micah and its place and thus its role between these two books about Nineveh, for however and whenever the books were composed and redacted, the final form of the text (Jonah, Micah, Nahum) is the order which Jews, Protestants and Catholics have in their canon and thus is the reading order for most. As well as covering the standard introductory issues, this work gives a reading of the three books, including a new reading of the book of Nahum. My hope in this introduction is that those who are new to these books will feel that they have enough knowledge and understanding to be able to start handling the texts themselves.

Unless otherwise stated, all quotations are from the NASB, a version which is more literal than some and thus makes it a little easier to see the underlying Hebrew. Where there are verse numbering differences between the English and Hebrew, I give the English. I use a simplified transliteration system for the few words of Hebrew that are used. When talking about the prophets Jonah, Nahum and Micah, I engage with them as they appear to be presented in the world of the text.

2

Jonah

Introduction

There are great tummies and empty tummies in the book of Jonah. The great fish swallows Jonah and the worm chews through a plant big enough to cover Jonah. At the opposite end of the spectrum, the animals in Nineveh are put on a fast and not allowed to eat or drink a thing, along with the humans. In fact, all the animals in Jonah have rather strange eating habits (Woods 2022: 165). The oddness in Jonah does not stop with the animals, however, and there is role reversal where the pagan sailors and the wicked Assyrian city of Nineveh behave more rightly than the Hebrew who fears God. In the quirky book of Jonah, the characters are greater than life and the language itself favours the word 'great'. Person (1996: 121) asserts that '"large" refers to only those things that have the LORD as their cause. [then as a footnote] That is, Nineveh, the wind, the storm, the sailors' fear, Jonah's anguish, the plant, Jonah's rejoicing.' Many have pointed to the book's humorous quality, but to focus solely on the humour or quirkiness would be to miss that Jonah has some serious messages to convey. Or to put it more in the language of the book itself, Jonah has a great proclamation to proclaim to you great readers.

Categorizing Jonah

Identifying Jonah

Jonah, the son of Amittai, is nowhere described in the book of Jonah as a prophet. The traditional approach, however, has been to equate him with the Jonah referred to in 2 Kgs 14.25 who is described as 'Jonah the son of Amittai, the prophet, who was of Gath-hepher'. Fretheim (1977: 30) comments that the link gives credibility to the Jonah of the book of Jonah as an established prophet, lest one suppose him to be a free-wheeling 'oddball or unbeliever'. Jesus refers to Jonah as a prophet in the New Testament (Mt. 12.39). Some early Jewish stories considered Jonah to be the deceased son of the widow of Zarephath who Elijah brought back to life (Torrey 1946: 27, translation 41–2). because of Amittai (a name based on the word for 'truth') and the widow attributing Elijah's words as 'true' (1 Kgs 17.24).

Locating Jonah in time and space

The setting of the story of Jonah is often linked with the perceived historical Jonah and since the setting of the Jonah mentioned in 2 Kgs 14.25 was the reign of Jeroboam II of the Northern Kingdom of Israel around 790–750 BCE (Goldingay 2021: 369 – the precise determining of dates in ancient history is not straightforward but most propose dates around this time), many have dated the story of Jonah to this period. One of the questions arising with a date of 790–750 is how much Assyria was a key presence in the region at that time. Stuart (1987: 432) warns of 'the supposedly erroneous identification of Nineveh as the actual royal capital of Assyria in Jonah's time', though Limburg (1988: 137) writes, 'During this period Nineveh was an important Assyrian city; from the time of Sennacherib (704 BC) it was the capital'. Goldingay (2021: 369) asserts that, at that time, 'Assyria and Nineveh were irrelevant to Israel. Neither is mentioned in earlier chapters of 2 Kings or in Amos'. Baldwin (1999: 545) points out that between 841 and 814/813 Jehu had become a vassal of Assyria and had to pay tribute to a foreign power for the first time. Then Adad-nērāri III (810–783) recorded that he had exacted recognition from Joash of Samaria 'and this could well have been an occasion for the exchange of diplomatic missions' (Wiseman 1979: 50). Coupled with famines in 765 and 759 (unless it was one famine that lasted from 765 to 759) and 'an ominous solar eclipse' in 763 (Wiseman 1979: 50), rebellions arose in various cities until 758. Wiseman (1979: 50) proposes that these rebellions could be the 'calamity and violence' (Jon. 3.8) which had come up before God and against which Jonah was to preach.

It has been suggested that Nineveh means 'house of fish' based on the cuneiform sign (the script used for writing Assyrian) for 'Nina', but this is a tenuous link with little evidence (see Hoyt 2018: 350 for further explanation) and many commentaries do not even mention it.

Scholars have been interested in Nineveh's place in the world in Jonah's day primarily because of trying to cast light on why Jonah did not want to go to Nineveh and witness God's mercy to them (the reason is not given in the text itself). The most appealing solution is that Jonah witnessed Assyria and thus Nineveh at the height of its cruelty and so he did not want such a wicked people to have God's forgiveness. Ultimately, though, even if a precise date could be given, it would not be possible to say with certainty why Jonah did not want to go to Nineveh, and fled to Tarshish instead.

Various possibilities have been given for the location of Tarshish, including Tarsus in Turkey, Rhodes in the Aegan, Carthage in North Africa, Sardinia between France and Italy, and Tarsus in Spain (Goldingay 2021: 381). Stuart (1987: 450–1) helpfully explains the situation. As a place name 'derived from the more basic meaning "sea"' (451), Tarshish was probably a name as common as Portland is in the United States (451). This would be because of its name being descriptive rather than a place name – as Portland means 'the land by a port'. Tarshish 'had the more basic meaning "open sea" or the like' and is where the phrase, 'ships of the open sea' originated (e.g. Isa. 23.1) (Stuart 1987: 451). The Targum translates Jon. 1.3 as 'in/on the sea' and Stuart himself is persuaded that Tarshish is not a place name but denotes the sea itself (451; see also Perry 2006: 84).

Some have seen Tarshish as 'a geographical metaphor for where YHWH is not known' (Trible 1996: 494; see also Watts 1975: 77) and is often denoted as the opposite direction to Nineveh (e.g. Trible 1996: 494; Goldingay 2021: 381; Nogalski 2023: 324). It is not Nineveh, however, from which Jonah is fleeing – it is God's presence – so to try to relate Tarshish to Nineveh, spatially, might be missing the point. The open sea with its overtones of chaos might be in Jonah's mind the opposite direction to God's presence. At the same time, it is likely that Tarshish was a long way from Jerusalem and its temple where God's presence was centred.

Authoring Jonah

Scholars have argued for both a late and an early date for the writing down of the story. Some of the attempts to provide an authorial date for Jonah have been based on analysing the language, such as putative Aramaisms suggesting a post-exilic context, or the reference to the king of Nineveh in ch. 3 indicating a time after the fall of the Assyrian Empire. Later studies have shown that neither of these suppositions are valid (Trible 1994: 465; see also Stuart 1987: 432), though Goldingay (2021: 370) sees the Aramaisms as having some weight, albeit not strong. Along with the later interest in Assyria, 'it fits the picture of a story that would make sense when told some centuries after Jonah's own day' (370). Hoyt (2018: 342) gives a tabular summary of the debated linguistic features. In summary, there has been no consensus and Trible (1994: 466) wryly comments, 'With no secure evidence to date Jonah, scholars have wandered through seven centuries to find it a home … Some critics still try to date Jonah, but others turn from the quest.' The book of Jonah has linguistic and literary connections with Jeremiah and Joel, but these have not afforded much help in terms of dating Jonah.

The psalm in Jonah 2 has created an extra layer of complexity to dating issues, primarily because it is so different from the rest of the book: it is a psalm amidst narrative; the language is different; and even the content seems skewed. Scholars have debated which came first – psalm or narrative – and whether the psalm inspired the rest of the book of Jonah or was added afterwards, and if so, whether it was inserted by the original author or by an editor. An example of the different language in Jonah 2 is demonstrated in the vocabulary, for example, that there is no reference to 'great' or 'evil/wickedness/misery' which are common across the rest of Jonah, and as Trible (1996: 505) points out, instead of the word that has been used for 'hurl' in ch. 1 – a word that Jonah himself uses in 1.12 – Jonah uses a different word in 2.3 – 'cast'. When it comes to content, Jonah makes no reference to his running from Nineveh and from God, but the elephant in the room is surely the fish, for Jonah does not mention it in his prayer.

Trible (1996: 464–5) gives a concise summary when she writes:

> Scholars who struggle with the status of the psalm have collected an arsenal of criteria by which to render judgment. It includes linguistics, genre, vocabulary, content, context, theology, structural design, plot development, and character portrayal. In the use of these criteria every point set forth

counters a counterpoint and every counterpoint a point. For instance, Vanoni argues against the original inclusion of the psalm because it speaks of deliverance while Jonah is in the belly of the fish; Limburg argues for the original inclusion of the psalm because it speaks of deliverance while Jonah is in the belly of the fish ... Critics on all sides of the issue use the same criteria to support opposite conclusions.
The traditional debate about the psalm appears to be at a draw.

It seems, nevertheless, that most scholars conclude that Jonah's prayer in Jonah 2 is a later addition by a different author. In the past thirty-five years there has been 'a resurgence of investigations attempting to explain Jonah as a composite book, even while seeing an increasing number of interpretations of Jonah as a unified composition' (Nogalski 2023: 294). Nogalski himself in 2011 (429) points out other places in the Hebrew Bible where a psalm occurs in the middle of narrative: the songs of Moses and Miriam in Exodus 15 following the crossing of the sea; Moses' song before his death in Deuteronomy 32; the song of Deborah (Judges 5); David's song of thanksgiving (2 Samuel 22); and Hezekiah's psalm (Isa. 38.9-20). Recent scholars arguing for a composite book tend towards a 'rolling-corpus model rather than a source-critical model' (Nogalski 2023: 295). At this point, we will move to Jonah's literary characteristics, not to further the discussion on when Jonah was authored, but to attempt to discover how the story is to be read.

Jonah's literary characteristics

Genre

Those who consider that the fish was a place from which Jonah needed deliverance rather than the fish itself being the deliverance, think that a psalm of lament would have been more appropriate in Jonah 2 than one of praise (e.g. Anderson 2000: 105). As Stuart (1987: 439) remarks, however, 'Once Jonah is inside the belly of the fish he has been delivered from drowning. A lament psalm would be appropriate only while he was still sinking in the Mediterranean. He *has* already experienced deliverance, and a thanksgiving psalm is the only sort appropriate to his situation'. The language of Jonah 2 resonates with various psalms, for instance: Sheol as the place of the dead (v. 2 cf. Pss. 6.5; 88.3, 5, 10-12; 139.8); the waters as a place of death (v. 3 cf. Pss.

42.7; 68.22; 69.2, 15); and the pit being a place of the dead (v. 6 cf. Ps. 16.10; 30.9). Nogalski (2023: 349) argues that Jonah's psalm reflects the standard pattern of an individual thanksgiving psalm, albeit that the introduction is muted because the psalm does not start with a summons to praise.

While the second chapter of Jonah stands in stark contrast to the rest of the book's narrative, the narrative of Jonah is unique among the prophetic books in that it primarily tells a story rather than is a compilation of oracular pronouncements. I use the word 'story' loosely to sidestep to some extent the issue of genre of Jonah, for the genre of Jonah has been debated and many options proposed: allegory, didactic story, fable, fairy tale, folktale, historical account, legend, Märchen, mašal, midrash, myth, novella, parable, parody, prophetic tale, saga, satire, sermon, short story and tragedy. Scholars such as Alexander (1988: 70) assure us that the difference is often minor and that the issue is more to do with finding the correct label.

One of the main reasons for the lack of support for a single label is that Jonah does not fit well with many of these terms. Douglas Stuart (1987: 435-7) and Phyllis Trible (1996: 467–74) explain some of the issues. Trible points out, for instance, that while the book of Jonah has the characteristics of folktales (royalty mixing with commoners, and the animal and human world freely mixing), folktales do not have the attributes of Jonah (an omnipotent deity who controls the plot). Nor are folktales rooted in a historical and geographical setting. Another example of a problematic genre is that of parable. First, Jonah is rather long for a parable, secondly, there is no explanation at the end and, thirdly, if one looks at Jonah in contrast to the parables in the Gospels, Jonah talks about God, whereas the Gospel parables talk about God in metaphors. Thus, to use Trible's words, 'Jonah is far too theological to be a parable' (1996: 469). In terms of satire, she asks, 'How much satire does the book yield and how much do readers contribute? Jonah may have both less and more levity and gravitas than readers intend' (1996: 471). Rather than trying to categorize Jonah in terms of genre, it is worth simply recognizing that the book incorporates various strands of different genres.

Bewer (1912: 4) writes that 'it is a sin against the author to treat as literal prose what he intended as poetry' and while most contemporary scholars would see the book of Jonah as likely to be a fictional account, not all draw this conclusion. Alexander and Stuart are scholars who offer some of the most persuasive arguments for Jonah being historical. Alexander, for instance, argues that 'the modern dictum, "If miraculous, unhistorical"'

(1988: 111) is imposed upon Jonah whereas the biblical author may well have viewed the improbable events as history. He observes:

> The author, if anything, actually plays down the miraculous nature of the various extraordinary events recorded in the narrative. Thus his description of Jonah being swallowed by the great fish is told in a very matter-of-fact manner, with no attempt being made to embellish the account with extravagant details. This seems remarkable, especially when we are asked to believe the author is fond of hyperbole. Whereas many modern expositions of Jonah tend to dramatize the events in a most unrealistic manner, the same is not true of the Hebrew original. (Alexander 1988: 72–3)

Those who argue for the historicity of Jonah refer to previous generations of scholars and interpreters (both Jewish and Christian) who believed that the events in Jonah 'actually occurred' (Alexander 1988: 74; see also Hoyt 2018: 357). They determine that the historicity is important to interpretation since, 'If it really happened, it is really serious' (Stuart 1987: 440). That is, historicity carries more weight than fiction.

It is entirely reasonable for those with faith to believe in a God of miracles while maintaining that the book of Jonah is fiction. Nevertheless, the issue is a pertinent reminder that readers' presuppositions affect their interpretation. Nogalski (2011: 401) rightly observes that 'modern scholars' assume the book of Jonah as fiction while lay people assume that it actually happened. While one's assumption affects the reading, most would probably agree with Nogalski (2011: 401) that 'the truth of the book, however, goes far deeper than historical questions'.

Bewer (1912: 10) addresses an issue that is still problematic to some over a hundred years later:

> Often this reference of Jesus to *the sign of Jonah* has been used as an argument for the historicity of the story of Jonah. Jesus believed in it, so it is reasoned, consequently His followers must do so also. But Jesus had no intention of affirming or denying its historicity. He was using an illustration, and an illustration may be drawn from fiction as well as from actual history.

Many would agree that genre or writing style does not determine historicity or otherwise (e.g. Goldingay 2021: 371), but would nevertheless use it as a guide. The literary reasons for deeming Jonah to be a work of fiction are the larger-than-life language in Jonah, the slightly humorous way of writing, the seemingly non-factual elements, and that the story ends with a question that functions as a punchline.

Larger-than-life language

'Jonah is a literary gem' (Trible 1996: 474) in terms of its language: repetition (Trible gives a good, concise breakdown of repeated words on pages 476–7), metaphor and larger-than-life scenarios. 'Great' is a word that is used frequently in Jonah (fourteen times in total) though, in the English versions, it is not always easy to see when the Hebrew word has been used. For instance, 'the king and his great *ones*' is the literal translation of Jon. 3.7, but most English translations would have something like 'the king and his nobles'. Or though the literal rendering of 1.10 is 'the men feared a great fear', it is likely to be translated along the lines of 'exceedingly afraid' (ESV and KJV), 'extremely frightened' (NASB), 'terrified' (NIV) or 'even more afraid' (NRSV). Nevertheless, it is possible to see even from the English the repetition of 'great', particularly in the first chapter (1.2, 4 [twice], 10, 12, 16, 17). Other instances occur in 3.2, 3, 5, 7; 4.1, 6, 11.

Another word that is common in Jonah is the word in Hebrew which can be translated variously in English, including 'wickedness/evil', but also 'disaster' and 'misery'. It is mentioned nine times in Jonah (1.2, 7, 8; 3.8, 10 [twice]; 4.1, 2, 6) and Stuart argues that the use in 1.2 is 'to describe the *troubles* [emphasis his] the city is having, not merely its evil ways' (1987: 437, see also 449). Thus, he argues, it is hinted at the outset that God cares about Nineveh and may have been the reason that Jonah wanted to run away.

Humour

Not everyone (e.g. Stuart) sees humour in Jonah, but many do, particularly in the third chapter, despite the serious nature of the city's actions. The humour often centres around the animals which are covered in sackcloth and made to fast, a seemingly ludicrous scenario. It has sometimes been said that animals were occasionally involved in mourning in Persian times and later, for example, Stuart (1987: 493) who references Herodotus, Plutarch and Jdt. 4.10, but Nogalski (2023: 374) rejects this contention (which he attributes to Kraeling) as 'forced' and coming from a single reference in Herodotus (9.24) which mentions the shearing of the head of man and beast. Wiseman (1979: 47) cites the *šumma ālu* (ancient omens about Mesopotamia written in Akkadian on clay tablets), some of which concentrate on the actions of animals at the time of a solar eclipse. At any rate, however, if animals were involved in mourning or solar eclipses, it was not to express repentance.

It is worth differentiating between, at least, the speakers in Jonah 3, the narrator/author(s) and the contemporary readers. The king, his nobles and the people speak and act in sincerity. They fast and wear sackcloth and ashes in the hopes that God may relent. That is serious, self-abasing and self-denying behaviour. Whether the narrator/author intended humour is another thing, however, and what one means by humour is also open to debate. The tone of Jonah throughout, with its exaggerated language, would indicate that the narrator is making the point in no uncertain terms – from the greatest, including the king, to the least, as far down as the animals. As well, there is wordplay in these verses. The word for 'edict'/'decree' in 3.7 is the noun of the verb 'taste' a few words later (3.7) and the word for 'eat'/'feed'/'pasture' (3.7) sounds like the word for 'evil'/'wicked' (3.8). Whether the author(s)/redactors cracked a smile while writing Jonah is something we will never know. It seems to me that the book of Jonah most certainly contains serious messages/content, but that there is also humour, but the book can be read with or without humour as contemporary commentators demonstrate. If the reader sees only humour in the book of Jonah, then that is, arguably, a thin reading. To see no humour in the book, however, I would argue, is to miss the fact that serious points can be made through humour.

Non-factual elements

Probably the most discussed and debated element of the story of Jonah in terms of factuality is the great fish and whether someone could live inside a fish for three days and three nights. Incidents where this is supposed to have happened have not been verified (despite claims to the contrary), but in many ways are irrelevant if one accepts the world of the Bible where miracles happen. In terms of the Bible, rather than the reader's own belief system, it is clear, given the parting of the Red Sea, the raising of the widow of Zarephath's son and numerous other miracles, that the God of the Old Testament could easily make Jonah live in a fish. Even if it is totally impossible for this to happen in 'real life', readers are obviously expected to take the text on its own terms and accept that it did for Jonah.

Jonah 3.3 makes a subsequent observation that Nineveh is 'a three days' walk'. This precise phrase is a *hapax legomenon* and thus difficult to translate (hence the slight variations across the modern English translations), but it seems clear that the phrase is to portray the size of Nineveh. Big cities even today are not a three-days' walk across them and a number of proposals have been suggested over the years, such as the circumference being a three-day walk (that still would not take three days), or that it would take three days for Jonah to preach properly in every area, or that a proper journey would include business and socializing as well as preaching, or that the text refers to an area larger than the city itself akin to 'Greater Nineveh' – cf. Gen. 10.11-12, where four places including Nineveh appear to be called 'the great city' (though this is perhaps unlikely since Jonah went outside the city and sat down to watch), or simply that the language is exaggerated (for these various options, see Bewer 1912: 50–2; Stuart 1987: 486–8; Cary 2008: 107; Erickson 2021: 370; Goldingay 2021: 396). Given that the book of Jonah is larger-than-life and that most of the other suggestions are problematic, the most plausible explanation is that the three days' walk is an example of exaggerated language employed to demonstrate the greatness of the city.

To our knowledge, there was no king of Nineveh (there was a king of Assyria) and Jonah 3 is the only time where the king of Nineveh is mentioned in the OT. Some scholars have suggested possible ways around this but again, given the book's exaggerated language, it is likely that the/a ruler of Nineveh has been described in more grandiose terms in the same way that his three-days-to-traverse city has been.

Structure and patterns

The structure can be presented as a simple summary of each of the book's four chapters: before Nineveh – the storm; in the fish – the psalm; at Nineveh – repentance; and after Nineveh's repentance – the plant and the worm. Trible gives a table showing the symmetry between the first and second halves of the book, starting with the word of the LORD that came to Jonah in 1.1 and the word of the LORD that came to Jonah a second time in 3.1 (1996: 475). Other patterns and structures have been suggested. Raymond Person's 1996 monograph is one such example where he explores what he terms 'adjacency pairs' in what amounts to be a high percentage of speech and conversation in the narrative, e.g. question/answer, request/refusal (12) – see 47–50 for the outline of the adjacency pairs.

Stuart (1987: 456–7) is scathing about what he calls the 'full discussion of words repeated in Jonah' that is given by Magonet and others and concludes,

The net result is overinterpretation. In Magonet's analysis (and those of similar studies) the book of Jonah ceases to be a simple narrative and becomes a complex vocabulary puzzle whose solution or even existence would never have occurred to any hearer or reader until the advent of the current fascination with complex rhetorical analysis. Magonet's patterns (hardly consistent) are of the type one would find in any narrative of a few chapters' length where sets of actions are described in simple terms.

He views chiastic structures similarly and while he does see patterns, he finds Fretheim's ABCCBA structure of Jon. 1.4-16 and others like it to be too 'elaborate' and 'forced'. Fretheim sees an ABCCBA chiasmus in the fourth chapter as well as the first (1977: 73, 117), but the majority of chiasms focus on Jonah 1; see, for instance, Hannah (1985: 1465) and Nogalski (2011: 411). Nogalski also sees a chiastic structure for part of ch. 2 (2011: 428).

In the OT, there are a number of places where God commissions someone to do his work. The structure of the story where someone is called often follows a pattern (on the various parts of a call narrative, see Habel 1965: 297–323). Jonah's call is abrupt and lacks any introductory words (the first few words of the book double up as both the superscription and Jonah's call), but one of the components of the call narrative is the person's objection to the call, usually for reasons of inadequacy. Jonah wastes no breath in liaising with God, however; he simply gets up and goes in the opposite direction. Perhaps he has grown up with the story of Moses and knows that resistance is futile. He may even have heard of how Elijah fled after the great miracle of fire falling from the sky and although God caught up with Elijah, perhaps Jonah thought that he could at least put some distance between himself and God. There are many parallels between Elijah and Jonah, which the rabbis and modern commentators have discussed, for example Perry (2006: 58–73) looks at the plant episode in Jonah 4 in relation to Elijah's epiphany.

Jonah through the ages

As has been seen already, particularly in the section on genre, scholars have read Jonah in different ways. Interpretations will be discussed in the course of discussion, but there is no dedicated section here on the history of interpretation. For those interested in the subject, the first chapter of Thomas Bolin's *Freedom beyond Forgiveness* (1997: 13–67) is an excellent survey of the field of Jonah studies, from pre-modern interpreters through to exegetes in the late 1990s. Tiemeyer's introduction to her commentary

(2022: 2–11) gives a shorter, but informative survey of Jewish, Christian and Islamic interpretation and her entire commentary is packed with legends, traditions, readings and interpretations of Jonah, as the title *Jonah Through the Centuries* would imply. Yvonne Sherwood has done a huge amount of research in her monograph, *A Biblical Text and Its Afterlives: The Survival of Jonah in Western Culture* (2000), to provide a comprehensive body of sources which have used Jonah. She critically walks through these materials spanning Jewish and Christian literature, secular texts, films and art, summarizing and evaluating them.

Jonah 1 – rising up to go down

The prophetic books begin with superscriptions which give, at the least, the name of the prophet (if that can be called a superscription at all) and often the time and place of the prophet's ministry. The book of Jonah begins with, 'The word of the Lord came to Jonah the son of Amittai' (Jon. 1.1) and thus has one of the shorter superscriptions. In fact, there is no real beginning to the book of Jonah because it starts with a conjunction (*waw* – 'and') as if it was continuing a story (in a way that we might say in English, 'And then' – 'And (then) the word of the Lord came to Jonah'). While Joshua, Judges, 1 Samuel, Ruth and Esther all begin with a conjunction, as Price and Nidor (1993: 49) point out, they start with an introductory, 'It came to pass' type clause, whereas the verb that starts with the conjunction in Jonah functions as a main verb.

The text rushes on with the command to 'Arise, go to Nineveh the great city and cry against it [feminine singular], for their [masculine plural] wickedness has come up before me' (Jon. 1.2). It is unusual for a prophet to go to a nation with his message, far less a foreign city, so Jonah's calling is unique. Obadiah, the book that precedes Jonah in the canon, is an oracle against a foreign nation, but Obadiah was not expected to go to Edom as far as we know. After Jonah is told to rise up and go to Nineveh, the text appears to race on with the word, 'So, Jonah rose up to …', but it becomes apparent that the *waw* conjunction in Hebrew is not to be translated 'So' after all, but 'But', for Jonah is not rising up to go to Nineveh, *but* rising up 'to flee to Tarshish from the presence of the Lord' (Jon. 1.2). The *waw* conjunction can be translated in a number of ways, the most frequent of which is 'And'.

Jonah 1.3 twice reports that Jonah is fleeing 'to Tarshish, from the presence of the Lord'. Limburg (1993: 43) observes that Cain is the only other person in the Bible who attempted to run away from the presence of the LORD (Gen. 4.16). While Elijah fled for his life, he did not run from the presence of the Lord. Stuart (1987: 450) considers that Jonah wanted to get away from where the LORD was worshipped, that is, away from Israel. Perry (2006: xxx) describes the problem 'as one of a threatened *relationship* [emphasis his] (between God and His messenger)'. In fact, Perry likens the relationship to an amorous one that is in trouble.

The partial explanation for why Jonah did not want to go to Nineveh is given in 4.2 – Jonah knew that God would forgive the Ninevites. Is there a reason the text does not specify this in ch. 1? It is unlikely to be a 'cliff-hanger' given that the reason is given three relatively short chapters later, and cliff-hangers only work for the first time of reading. In addition, it does not seem a dramatic-enough point to be held back. It might be that the narrator wants to focus on Jonah's response rather than the reason behind it. Another possibility is that when we are told, it is by means of direct speech from Jonah and Jonah has not yet spoken. To have Jonah speaking from the outset would give a different tone to the story where his lack of speech speaks loudly and emphasizes his actions. Jonah's confession in 4.2 is also better placed there because of the irony in Jonah's utterance, having escaped death himself by that point. It may even be a combination of all these reasons.

In the OT, the idea of turning/repentance is an important theme which is conveyed by the transliterated word *shuv* (which can mean 'turn', 'return' or 'repent'). Jonah's rising and fleeing is like an oppositive of *shuv*. He is the antithesis of the repentant person and in refusing the task, Jonah stands alone, for no other prophet disobeyed God's commission; Moses arguably refused when he asked God to send someone else, but he went with Aaron. While the book of Jonah starts in a hurried manner, Jonah temporarily brings the story to a standstill. It takes two chapters for the story to start again.

When God 'visits' humans in the OT, he comes 'down' (e.g. when his glory came down on Mount Sinai in Exod. 18.19, 20) and God was seen to be dwelling 'up' in the heavens. To go in the opposite direction to God's presence, therefore, is to go 'down' and this is what Jonah does – twice in Jon. 1.3 – he goes down to Joppa and then down into the ship. In that sense, Jonah is running away from God's presence on two planes: horizontally (to Tarshish) and vertically (down).

In 1.3, Jonah pays 'her [the ship's] fare/hire/wages', which is normally translated as Jonah paying his fare, but this is unusual language and is normally used for paying a person, rather than a ship. Ginzberg's *Legends of the Jews* ([1913] 2003: 1031) shows that since earliest times, some have seen Jonah as paying for the entire ship/cargo.

As easy as it might have been for Jonah to flee from the LORD at the outset – all the resources he needs seem to be on hand – it soon changes. The LORD hurls a great wind onto the sea. The animals, weather and even inanimate objects play significant roles in the book of Jonah and in Jon. 1.4, the ship 'devised' to break up. This may be wordplay, because the words for 'devising/thinking' and 'breaking up' sound similar, but 'it is a vivid word he uses, for it represents the ship as an animate being, agitated, full of fear, lit., *it thought it would be broken in pieces*' (Bewer 1912: 32; see also Limburg 1993: 27, 48–9). Limburg adds, 'The Hebrew gives "the ship" some extra emphasis here, again placing the subject before the verb. The Masoretic punctuation also emphasizes the word, making a pause after "ship"; thus a literal reading, "and as for the ship – it had a mind to break up"' (1993: 49). Inanimate objects are not the subject of this verb elsewhere in the OT as inanimate objects are not the recipients of 'fare/hire/wages'. It may be an over-reading to translate the ship as the subject of the active verb, but nevertheless, given the tone of Jonah overall, it is worth considering. To explain briefly Limburg's reference to the 'Masoretic punctuation': in about the sixth/seventh to tenth centuries CE, the Masoretes added vowels, accents and punctuation to the existing Hebrew text which consisted of consonants only. The resulting 'Masoretic Text' (MT) is the Hebrew version underlying most of our English translations of the Bible.

In 1.5, the sailors each pray to their gods and frantically hurl (the same word used for God hurling a great wind) utensils into the sea. The text seems to imply that they threw the things into the sea to lighten the ship, but the sailors might have intended to make an offering to the gods who control the seas (Trible 1996: 495–6). The Hebrew has, 'in order to make light from upon them' (Hebrew often doubles up prepositions), or to smooth it out a little, 'in order to make it lighter for them'. This has sometimes been interpreted to mean to lessen their danger (e.g. Price and Nida 1993: 56). Some argue that throwing cargo overboard in a storm to make the boat ride higher is bad nautical practice (e.g. Trible 1996: 495–6), though Bolin (1997: 79–80) cites other examples of incidences of lightening the ship in this way in storms.

While God and the sailors are hurling things around, Jonah, has 'gone down' into the ship and is fast asleep. The contrast between Jonah's behaviour with his seeming lack of fear and that of the sailors is remarkable. Is Jonah's sleeping a spiritual torpor in contrast to that of the sailors' prayers? Or has Jonah given up and resigned himself to whatever God is going to throw at him, even if the ultimate destiny down is Sheol? Trible (1996: 518) asks if it was because he knows that God will rescue him. Or might it be that Jonah is, for the moment, where he wants to be and there is no reason for his sleep to be disturbed?

The verb for sleep suggests a deep sleep, a hypnotic sleep (a noun from the same root is used for Adam's deep sleep in Gen. 2.21) or a sleep that precedes death (Stuart 1987: 454, 458; Trible 1996: 496; Limburg 1993: 50; Perry 2006: 6), though the chief of sailors evidently is able to wake up Jonah and recall him to life. So far nothing has threatened Jonah's going down, away from the presence of God – not even the storm or the ship threatening to break up. His deep sleep is just another unconscious step in the right direction for Jonah, but the 'deep sleep' that precedes death is the first warning bell to readers that Jonah's going down away from God is increasingly separating himself from life.

The command the captain gives Jonah starts in the same manner as the one God gave him at the start; arise and call/cry, but whereas God told Jonah to cry against Nineveh (1.2), the captain instructs him to call on his God. Person contrasts the sailors (1.14) and the Ninevites (3.6, 8), who call out without needing prompting or coercion, with Jonah who resists, despite being commanded to do so by both God (1.2-3) and the sailors (1.6). He does, however, without prompting, call out to God from inside the fish in 2.3 (Person 1996: 72, 87). The sailors' message unwittingly, as Alexander (1988: 103) points out, mocks Jonah with its echo of God's call. There is no indication that Jonah followed the captain's orders; in fact to come into God's presence in prayer would be to negate the very reason he is on the ship.

The sailors cast lots to determine whose fault the storm is. While the OT does not go into much detail about casting lots, it records without comment the practice and its outcome and Prov. 16.33 and 18.18 seem to approve its use. Given that Jonah had told his shipmates that he was fleeing from the LORD (1.10), it is somewhat surprising that they do not suspect him, but perhaps they do, and the lots confirm it.

In answer to their questions, Jonah refers to himself (1.9) as a Hebrew. This is an unusual appellation for one might expect the description of Israelite or even Judahite, but it might be that 'Hebrew' was used by foreigners or to foreigners (Price and Nidar 1993: 61). Interestingly and ironically, the first words that Jonah utters are credal, with the affirmation that he fears the LORD God of heaven who made the sea and the dry land. Erickson (2021: 257) makes the interesting observation that Jonah did not list 'a downward realm' when he lists heaven, sea and dry ground as part of God's domain. Unsurprisingly, some commentators have been critical of Jonah's confession (von Rad [1960] 1975: 291, Limburg 1993: 59, Baldwin

1999: 560), but it need not be read so negatively. Jonah has not volunteered this information; he is simply responding to a question with the truth. He is an authentic servant of the LORD, which is perhaps why the word of the LORD came to him in the first place. Most faithful adherents of any religion have times when they have 'behaved badly' according to the tenets and precepts of that religion, without that behaviour negating their fundamental religious persuasion. In fact, this is arguably one of the central theological aspects of the book.

Jonah's declaration in 1.9 seems to imply that Jonah knows exactly who is causing the great storm that is buffeting the ship. Perry (2006: 104) observes that Jonah is the only character to say that he fears; the narrator is the one who tells us about the fears of the others. In v. 5, the sailors fear for their lives, it appears, but after Jonah's revelation they fear greatly. Is the increased fear due to realizing that this is not a random act of the gods, but a specifically honed and personalized act of God towards one man?

When Jonah tells the sailors to 'lift me up' and 'hurl me into the sea' (v. 12), the word 'hurl' is that used for God hurling the great wind on the sea and the sailors hurling their cargo into it. The word 'hurl' is used fourteen times in the Bible, four of which are in this chapter (Price and Nida 1993: 54). Everyone is intent on hurling things into the sea in this chapter.

Jonah knows God in a way that the sailors do not. He is confident that the sea will become calm and the sailors will be saved. Jonah could rise up and call on his God, a God who, if he made the sea and land, could easily stop the storm, but he will not rise. Others will have to lift him up and hurl him over the side of the ship even if they have his blood on their hands. Jonah's refusal to engage actively with the storm is his continued defiance towards God: Jonah will not respond to God and will not be forced by God to respond by whatever means God may choose to communicate. He is, however, willing to sacrifice his life in order that the sailors do not lose theirs on account of him. If the sea kills him as it looks certain to do, then Jonah will have lost his life, but he will not have gone to Nineveh as God wanted. The outcome will at least have been stalemate (see also Ginzberg's *Legends* (2003: 248); Trible 1996: 499; Watts 1975: 81).

Person points out that in the same way that Jonah did not vocally respond to God's request to go to Nineveh, but simply acted in a way that was contrary to the request/command, so the sailors do not answer Jonah with words, but act differently. That is, they still try to get to shore without throwing Jonah overboard (Person 1996: 147). Trible, Bewer and others have commented that steering towards shore is the wrong thing to do with a ship when there is a storm, but Bewer implies that they prefer 'being wrecked upon the reefs of the dangerous coast line' rather than risk the open sea in the current storm (Bewer 1912: 39).

In attempting to get to shore without killing Jonah, the sailors pray to the LORD (twice using his personal name YHWH), but as Trible (1996: 488) points out, there is no indication that the sailors stop worshipping their own gods or 'convert' to Jonah's faith. Cary suggests that it is through Jonah that the sailors know about the LORD and that in pointing them to his God, Jonah is doing his job as a prophet (Cary 2008: 68). Nevertheless, it is ironic that these pagan sailors are the ones who call on Jonah's God. To drown in a storm would be bad, but at least it would not carry the moral weight of murder that might be a fate worse than death. Stuart reasons that they probably fear that the God who had stirred up the storm against Jonah might turn against them if they do something to his prophet, not to mention humans avenging Jonah's death (1987: 463).

When God hurled a great wind to the sea in v. 4, a great tempest ensued and when the sailors hurl Jonah to the sea (the same language), the sea ceases its raging. Each time the verb 'hurl' is used in this chapter (vv. 4, 5, 12, 15), the context is the sea and each of the main actors or group of actors initiates it: God, the sailors and Jonah.

The word 'raging' (v. 15) is used elsewhere in relation to people, so the sea, like the boat, is a subject of an active verb usually used of humans. As Bewer remarks, 'The term used here makes the sea animate' (1912: 40). The boat and the sea are perhaps subtle foils for Jonah, for they appear to be acting in line with God's purposes.

Some have seen Jonah's being thrown into the sea as human sacrifice (e.g. Watts 1975: 81), but the text does not imply this and the OT condemns human sacrifices in other places (e.g. Deut. 18.9-12; Jer. 7.31, 19.5, 32.35; Ezek. 16.20-21, 23.37). There is nothing to suggest that Jonah was not an orthodox prophet. His utterances about and to God sum up nicely the character of God and it is unlikely that he should think that his death would be considered an acceptable sacrifice to God. Rather, the sea was the only option. The sailors do not see it as a human sacrifice for they ask God to spare them having Jonah's blood on their hands.

When the sailors see that the God of the sea and dry land has calmed the storm, they again fear with a great fear, but this time it is God whom they greatly fear. Their fear which was generalized/non-specific in v. 10 has been channelled by v. 16. Jonah's fear of God is surpassed by the sailors' great fear of him and Jonah's defiance to God is contrasted by their making sacrifices and vows to him. The sailors have behaved as the Hebrew prophet should have done. Making vows indicates that the sailors were intending some kind of longer-term commitment to Jonah's God.

Jonah 1.17 tells us that God appointed a great fish to swallow Jonah. 'And', 'But' or 'Now' is how most versions translate the beginning of 1.17, if they translate it at all, since the word acts like punctuation to start a new sentence. An equally valid and arguably more appropriate way to translate it, however, is 'So', for the great fish that swallowed Jonah was a direct answer to the sailor's prayers that they not be accountable for Jonah's blood and also in response to their sacrifices and vows. For this reason, it makes sense to split the chapter in the way that the Protestant versions have it and keep 1.17 as the last verse in ch. 1, rather than putting it as the first verse of ch. 2 as Jewish and Catholic versions do. Thus the beginning of 1.17 is translated, 'So the LORD appointed a great fish to swallow Jonah.' Watts (1975: 82) speaks for many commentators when he claims that 1.17 'belongs more to what follows than to what has passed', but there seems to be no reason for this logic. Perhaps there is an inherent disinclination to God answering the prayers of those not his people? As well as being an answer to the sailors' prayers, the saving of Jonah also takes the situation out of stalemate. Jonah is still alive and thus his arising and going to Nineveh is still an issue between God and Jonah. Thankfully for Jonah, the fish obeyed God's appointment and did not go in a different direction when God called it with something akin to, 'Arise, go to Jonah – he needs rescuing.'

Jonah 2 – inside the he-fish-she-fish

As stated above, the origins of the psalm in Jonah 2 have evoked much debate. The authorial/editorial intention is seen differently, depending on one's position on when the psalm was included. For instance, Nogalski (2023: 298) concludes that the psalm was an editor's attempt to portray Jonah more favourably than he is elsewhere in the book by inserting an existing thanksgiving psalm. Trible writes in 1996 (465), 'Current thinking poses the question differently. It does not ask if the psalm is an insertion; instead, it asks how the psalm functions in the story.' Such questions are less concerned with authorial and editorial intention, though obviously not divorced from them. One of the debates regarding Jonah's psalm in ch. 2 is whether it expresses a genuine sentiment and what its tone is. There are problems with the psalm in that it lacks humility, there is no repentance, and Jonah does not address his own part in the calamity, nor mention sin. He is a far cry from the Prodigal Son of Lk. 15.11-32. At the same time, such an attitude seems fitting for a prophet who has not yet made it off the starting block. As well, Jonah is never untruthful in the text, for example, he tells the sailors who he is and what he is doing, which is another reason to consider his prayer as uttered in sincerity. Jonah is not the model prophet – or psalmist. Nevertheless, the LORD is still 'his God'. Jonah has run from his God, the God he fears, and he has refused to engage him, but he has not denied him.

The first thing the reader learns when Jonah prays is that this is not his first prayer. He had previously prayed for deliverance from the belly, or womb, of Sheol (a different word to that used for the 'belly' of the fish and one frequently translated 'womb'). Price and Nida (1993: 54) comment that while Sheol is anthropomorphized in other ways, this is the only place in the OT where Sheol is described as having a belly/womb. In this original prayer, Jonah recounts that he had gone down into Sheol (2.2) and to the foundations of the mountains (2.6). Like many of the psalms as well as the book of Jonah itself, Jonah's prayer is highly metaphorical. It is entirely plausible that Jonah may have had breakers sweep over him and weeds wrapped around his head; it is not realistic for a number of reasons that he could have descended to the bottom of the sea as is implied by his descending to the 'roots of the mountains' (even if he was the Ancient Near Eastern free-diving record holder). Jewish sources have offered ways by which Jonah could have taken a tour of the sea and its bed, and Ginzberg (2003: 1033) relates the legend as if God or the fish had arranged a tour for Jonah of the lowest parts of the earth:

> The eyes of the fish served Jonah as windows, and, besides, there was a diamond, which shone as brilliantly as the sun at midday, so that Jonah could see all things in the sea down to its very bottom ... To show his gratitude [for Jonah saving him from the leviathan], the fish carried Jonah whithersoever there was a sight to be seen. He showed him the river from which the ocean flows, showed him the spot at which the Israelites crossed the Red Sea, showed him Gehenna and Sheol, and many other mysterious and wonderful places.

The full story of Jonah in Ginzberg's *Legends* makes compelling reading.

Jonah's claim that God had cast him into the deep (2.3) when he himself had told the sailors to throw him overboard may not be as strange as it seems at first glance; God took him down further than Jonah could have taken himself. Jonah has learnt that he could not flee God's presence by going down because God simply followed him down and then took – or sent – him down even further. Jonah is the worked example of Ps. 139.8-10, 'If I make my bed in Sheol, behold, You are there.' It seems that, at some point, Jonah has a change of heart (perhaps due to panic and physical distress) and there is a sense in which he is concerned that he has gone down too far and beyond the point of no return – to Sheol where God is out of reach. Jonah's metaphor undoubtedly parallels his physical and spiritual condition.

Jonah's statement that he had been driven away from before God's eyes (2.4) also seems bizarre given that we have heard twice in the previous chapter that Jonah is explicitly fleeing from God's presence. Trible (1994: 171) wryly comments that when Jonah does call to God, 'he misrepresents the situation'. Misrepresentation is not the only way to see the statement, however. Has Jonah's running away created such a breach in relationship that God has now rejected Jonah? Has Jonah's knowledge that God is gracious and compassionate led him to presume that God would not forsake him, whereas having cold water poured over him has brought him to his senses and he realizes that he cannot play fast and loose with the God who created this powerful sea (albeit a calm sea once he hit it) and the dry ground? Or is it simply the panicking of a man about to drown?

If one takes Jonah's prayer at face value, it demonstrates that when all is stripped away and Jonah is literally at rock bottom (according to his non-literal metaphors) and trapped by the earth's bars and the seaweed, Jonah does indeed fear and trust in the God of the waves and the breakers. What he told the sailors was the truth. His prayer for rescue is almost an automatic and deep-seated response from a man of faith who realizes that he does not, after all, want to be separated from God's presence. He has resisted God until the point when the alternative was the belly of Sheol. Jonah is totally reliant on God bringing up his life from the pit and cries out – 'and you heard my cry' (Jon. 2.2). This is the point at which Jonah addresses God in the second person, having started his prayer in the third person. God reverses the direction of movement thus far and brings Jonah up (2.6) for which Jonah is grateful and in ch. 3 he rises up of his own accord when commanded.

Yet Jonah was in the belly of the fish three days and three nights before he prayed to his God. Did he lie down and go to sleep as he had in the boat? Did he have another change of heart once he realized that he was safe, surmising that God would probably insist that he go to Nineveh? Was he waiting for

God to make the first move? Landes (1967: 448–50) considers that the three days and three nights that Jonah was in the fish before he prayed are akin to a Sumerian myth where it takes three days to go the underworld and back. Alexander (1988: 112) disagrees on the basis that there is 'insufficient evidence within the Old Testament itself to demonstrate that this is how a Hebrew reader would have interpreted the phrase'. Others (e.g. Watts 1975:82–3) have commented that three days after death is a period that ensures that someone could not come back to life (cf. Lazarus's four days in the tomb in John 11). The New Testament draws a parallel between Jonah's time of three days and three nights in the belly of the fish with Jesus' time in the grave (Mt. 12.40). Elizabeth Harper (2002: 461) writes, 'Sheol is the place of death, not birth … Yet always in Jonah the impossible and the improbable are the reality.' Perhaps it is in praying that Jonah goes from death to life and with the prayer is reborn in the womb of the fish.

Interestingly, the male noun for 'fish' is used for the fish that swallows Jonah, but when he prays from within the fish, the female version of 'fish' is used, leading some to see the fish's 'belly' as the womb. The fish that spews him out onto dry land is, again, a male fish. Early rabbinic literature does not pick up on this (Kadari 2016: 107), but a late midrash, the *Midrash of the Repentance of Jonah the Prophet* that 'circulated in northern France in the eleventh century' (Kadari 2016: 108), recites an aggadic tradition whereby Jonah is too comfortable in the male fish to pray, so after three days God causes him to be spewed into the mouth of a female fish full of young. Later a male fish swallows the female with Jonah inside. The mediaeval exegete Rashi uses this tradition in his commentary on Jonah. 'Midrash' and 'aggadah' are Jewish terms. A midrash is a (normally ancient) rabbinic close reading, or interpretation of the biblical text that pays careful attention to the little details that are in (and absent from) the text. An aggadah is a writing, often a legend or parable, on a non-legal text.

As Kadari notes, the swapping between male and female terms is not a problem in biblical Hebrew and follows Ibn Ezra in his Jonah commentary that multiple fish are unnecessary (Kadari 2016: 112). Nevertheless, she admits that this aggadic tradition highlights God's involvement in Jonah's life, not least in the miracles that kept him alive (and passing through three different fish is a way of drawing this out). It also emphasizes Jonah's unwillingness to pray until he is really desperate. 'The theological message of this midrash is that the divine plan will unfold, in spite of Jonah's behaviour, and ultimately with his consent' (Kadari 2016: 112–13). Tiemeyer (2017: 315–22) persuasively argues that the letter *heh* on the end of the male word for 'fish' does not turn it into the feminine variant, but rather is used because the word is in pause, pausal forms often utilizing longer variants. Pausal forms are used at the end of clauses when the natural tendency of speech is to lengthen the stressed syllable of the final word before a slight pause.

Trible (1996: 507, 508) points out that in the eight verses of Jonah's prayer to God, Jonah uses the first-person singular twenty-six times and 'none of these references is self-effacing; they are all boastful' (508). Indeed, no sooner is Jonah rescued than he is apparently self-righteously denouncing those who worship 'vain idols' and comparing them unfavourably with himself who will make sacrifices and vows (2.8-9). This is particularly ironic given that it was the sailors (those following vain idols) who offered sacrifices and made vows before Jonah had even submitted to the God from whom he was fleeing. At the same time, the final words of 2.8 read, literally, 'abandon/forsake their loving-kindness' which may imply that Jonah is thinking of fellow Hebrews who abandon God for idols, rather than inhabitants of the foreign nations. Alexander (1988: 117) sees it as a straightforward contrast: 'those who worship idols will discover in times of trouble how impotent they really are and as a result will no longer show loyalty, or love, to their supposed gods. Those who worship the LORD, however, will always find him trustworthy and reliable'. That is, Jonah is contrasting the gods, rather than favourably comparing himself to idol worshippers. Nevertheless, if the Prodigal Son is the ideal of the repentant sinner, Jonah is a demonstration that it is not only the ideal repentant person who is rescued.

Even if Jonah does not repent and he lacks humility, his first thoughts appear to be on worship – he wants to look to God's holy temple (2.4) – the central place of worship and God's presence. Nineveh and Tarshish are, at the moment, not in the picture. Having been rescued from the belly of the grave, Jonah is being recentred; his internal compass is being calibrated – perhaps a three-day process? It is interesting that 2.4 focuses on sight and looking, and that being cast from before God's eyes is equated with not being able to look at the temple. Implied is that, in a healthy relationship, both God (through His holy temple) and humans are in view of each other.

It is worth noting that while some versions (e.g. NIV) say that Jonah's prayer 'rose' to God's holy temple in v. 7, the Hebrew actually says, 'my prayer came to you, to your holy temple' (my translation) – the word for 'arise' that is used elsewhere in Jonah is not the word used here. Nevertheless, the scenario easily lends itself to imagining Jonah's prayer bubbling up from the depths of the sea. Verse 9 pictures Jonah inside the temple, offering sacrifices with thanksgiving and making good his vows. Either Jonah's prayer ends with a declaration that salvation belongs to the LORD, or God interrupts at this point, possibly in response to Jonah's prayer, although God does not address Jonah. God speaks to the fish (the male noun for 'fish' is used), which responds to God's words and vomits Jonah onto dry land (v. 10).

'Salvation is from the LORD' carries theological weight. The issue is not for whom salvation is but from whom salvation comes. Jonah is part of a people who have a special relationship with God, but that relationship does not mean that God's salvation belongs exclusively to them. His salvation may go beyond expected boundaries – to the foreign sailors and Ninevites, for instance.

When the sailors made sacrifices and vows, God appointed the fish to swallow Jonah, and when Jonah promises to make sacrifices and vows, God commands the fish to vomit him out, though there is no mention of Jonah actually making the sacrifices or vows. With the feminine noun for fish being used previously and Jonah having been in its belly/womb, Jonah's being vomited onto dry ground may be seen as a kind of birth. When Jonah is introduced in ch. 1, he is Jonah, son of Amittai. By the end of ch. 2, we might mischievously think of him as Jonah (meaning 'dove'), son of a fish. The Islamic commentator, Al Tabarī (838–923) considers that 'the whale … ejected Jonah onto the shore, and cast him up as if he were a newborn child fully preserved' (1987: 165). Christian iconography and paintings have also shown Jonah as naked or semi-naked (Sherwood 2000: 148 (L), (P) – plates between pages 148 and 149; Horne and Bewer 1909: 'The Sea-Monster Releases Jonah'). Erickson's work (2021: 310–13) has an excursus on the birth imagery in Jonah's psalm.

Jonah does not mention the fish in his prayer – does he even know he is inside a fish? (see also Stuart 1987: 475). Bewer (1912: 22) surmises that the fish 'did not seem so important to the writer as it does to us'. Jonah's prayer, as we have seen, however, does not include many of the elements that we might have expected. Instead, what is recorded is an uncluttered emphasis on his own position and God's salvation, a point that will be developed in the next chapter. The great fish, the great storm and even Jonah's running away grow strangely dim – at least for these few verses – in the light of God's deliverance of Jonah from certain death. Or to use Perry's words, 'humans do not pray in a place; rather, the Place is where they pray…At the highest level the true, the only "place of prayer" is *hammaqom*, God, *the Place*' (2006: 119).

Jonah 3 – an evangelist's dream, but Jonah's nightmare

Jonah 3 starts in exactly the same way as Jonah 1 – 'The word of the LORD came to Jonah'. As Limburg and others comment, 'Only Jonah among the biblical prophets has to have his assignment given to him twice' (Limburg 1993: 75). The instruction is the same, too, at least to begin with – 'Arise, go to Nineveh the great city and cry…' There is a slight departure at this point, which maybe just a difference in words, but in ch. 1, Jonah was to 'cry against' Nineveh, whereas here in ch. 3, he is to 'cry to' it. Perry (2006: 44) deems the difference to be 'enormous: the first projects impending destruction, whereas the second can mean even "*beg them* to repent" (Jon. 1.6, 14; 2.3; 1 Kgs 8.52)'. Indeed, in ch. 3, God says nothing about the wickedness of the great city. As in the first chapter, Jonah arises, but this time he rises to go to Nineveh. Had Jonah been the ideal prophet, the book of Jonah would be condensed to just one chapter.

Jonah acts 'in accordance with the LORD's word' and Stuart (1987: 483) remarks, 'Whether Jonah liked it or not, he went. And there is nothing here to suggest that Jonah liked it any more this time than the first.' Goldingay (2021: 396) notes that the phrase 'in accordance with the LORD's word' is only used on two other occasions of prophets (as opposed to others such as kings) in the OT. First, in the 2 Kgs 14.25 reference to Jonah and secondly of Elijah (1 Kgs 17.5).

This is not the only instance in the OT where God's word will not be thwarted. Like an armoured hero in an action film who takes a shot to the chest, falters for a second or two, and then just keeps on coming, so does God's word. In Jeremiah 36, when Jehoiakim burnt the scroll of God's words, God simply tells Jeremiah, 'Take another scroll and write' (Jer. 36.28). In Jonah, God takes the same prophet. Limburg notes that the Jonah story testifies to the power of God's word, and he lists the number of times the Hebrew word for 'word' in these few verses is used, including the underlying word translated in English versions as 'tell' or 'give' in 3.2 – 'the message which I am going to tell you' (1993: 81). The end of the book explains why the word/message is so important: God had compassion on Nineveh.

When Nineveh is first mentioned, it is with the epithet 'the great city' (1.2) and this is how she is described when the narrative resumes, post-fish (3.2). In fact, the text goes further and while 3.2 describes her as a 'great city',

3.3 informs us that 'Nineveh was a great city to God' (literal translation). The phrase 'great to God' is used only once in the OT. Most English versions translate this phrase as 'an exceedingly great city', but some have argued that the literal translation should not be smoothed out (e.g. Bewer 1912: 50; Stuart 1987: 486–7; Hoyt 2018: 477; Alexander 1988: 119; Trible 1996: 511). Fausset (n.d.: 579), on the other hand, regards it simply as an idiom since 'all greatness was in the Hebrew mind associated with God'. Trible contends that the phrase means that Nineveh

> impresses even God (great before God). It suggests divine ownership: God rules over Nineveh (great to God). It suggests divine favor: God has ordained the greatness of Nineveh (great because of God). And it suggests divine abode: The greatness of Nineveh qualifies as a residence for God (great for God). The theological greatness of the city exceeds a mere superlative. Human calculations do not suffice; divine standards take the measure. (1996: 511)

It seems unlikely that the greatness of Nineveh 'impresses' God, not least because her wickedness has come up before him. Also, contra to Trible, there is nothing to suggest that the city qualifies as a residence for God, nor does Trible explain why she considers that this might be the case, other than translating the *lamed* preposition as 'for' rather than 'to' (the latter indicating possession to her). Although Nineveh's size is unlikely to be what makes her great/important to God – if 'great to God' is not hyperbolic language in itself – it is unusual for the OT to express a city's greatness in terms of how big it is – a three-day journey (see earlier for discussion on this); one might expect to hear how many horses, ships, gold, silver or spices it had, but Jonah is full of unusual phrases. Given that material possessions are often indicative of God's blessing in the OT, for example, Abraham, Job, David and Solomon, Nineveh's greatness is more likely to be seen as a blessing from God rather than a cause of his interest.

If Nineveh is a city that is important to God, then it is a theological statement, for it means that a Gentile city (even a wicked one) is important to God. Limburg (1993: 76) states: 'The repeating of this assignment … hammers the point home; God cares about the peoples of the world, be they Ethiopians, Philistines (Amos 9.7), Egyptians – or Assyrians (Isa. 19.23–24).' As he also notes a little later (77), Nineveh is mentioned by name seven times in Jonah 3 (vv. 2, 3 twice, 4, 5, 6, 7). This is another reversal in the story: the sailors have behaved like righteous Israelites and now the pagan, wicked city is 'great' to God. The text is as quietly subversive as Jonah's act of fleeing God.

At this point, however, it is worth emphasizing along with most contemporary commentators that Jonah is not to be seen as representative of Jewish people who behave badly while Gentiles behave in an exemplary manner. That is, Christian readers have sometimes read themselves into the well-behaved Gentiles in Jonah, which can quickly lead to an anti-Semitic interpretation. The book of Jonah is part of the Hebrew Bible, told, written and compiled by Jewish people. If part of the point in the book of Jonah is that the outsiders shame the insiders, then it is a lesson in humility for all readers. It is not a general 'showing up' of insiders by outsiders, however. It is the specific story of a person of faith not living up to, nor wanting to live up to, a calling because the 'cost of discipleship' is deemed too high, and when the answer to God's commission is, 'Not this time'. Perhaps those who identify most with Jonah are people of faith (primarily those worshipping the God of Abraham, Isaac and Jacob) who are running from, not to, God in some way – those who can genuinely affirm credal statements and yet whose actions might be at some odds with them.

The hyperbolic three-day walk to cross the city is probably akin to a contemporary person describing a mansion house as having a drive 'a hundred miles long'. The speaker would not expect an analysis of the drive perhaps winding round and round the house in a tight spiral shape, coiled up like a liquorice Catherine wheel totalling 100 miles in length, or a discussion of whether it went outside the property for a long way before coming back in. To use Wolff's words, 'The reader is not supposed to do arithmetic. He is supposed to be lost in astonishment' (1986: 148). Is it significant that a person could traverse Nineveh in the time that Jonah was in the fish? Does the text want to make the point that Jonah could have gone to Nineveh, done his preaching and be on his way home again had he obeyed God? It is somewhat odd to have a description of how long it takes to get across Nineveh when, as countless others have pointed out, Nineveh is hundreds of miles inshore and yet there is no explanation of how Jonah got from the fish to Nineveh and how long that journey took.

The start of Jon. 3.4 is not entirely clear with the Hebrew text reading, literally, 'And/now Jonah began to go into the city, one day's walk'. NASB has 'Then Jonah began to go through the city one day's walk', while the NIV has 'On the first day, Jonah started into the city' and the NRSV, 'Jonah began to go into the city, going a day's walk.' Had Jonah just started the journey into the city or had he got one day's walk into it? Commentators make their proposals, but what is clear is that Jonah was at or near the start of his expected three-day journey.

Jonah proclaims (or 'calls') his message, which is, literally, 'Yet forty days and Nineveh will be overturned' (my translation). Most comment on the oddness of the message. First, it is short – five words in Hebrew – perhaps demonstrating, if it is not the headline of a much longer discourse, that while Jonah is obeying God, he is doing the least he can. Secondly, it was not the usual oracle couched in terms such as 'thus says the LORD', which is employed even in foreign nation oracles. Neither is there any mention of God. Thirdly, it gives no reason to the Ninevites – were they expected to know their own sins? Fourthly, it is also highly unusual that a prophecy should be given a time scale. Scholars have debated the 'forty days', which are rendered 'three days' in the LXX. Some have suggested that forty days gives the people time to repent, while others have argued the opposite. For a summary of the textual and interpretative issues of the three and forty, see Moberly's paper 'Preaching for a Response' (2003: 156–68). He concludes that forty days appeals to the human trait of procrastination in the hopes that the Ninevites would leave it too late (167). It is likely that the original Israelite/Judean audience, as today's, would hear 'multiple implications' (Stuart 1987: 489) when they heard the number forty.

Commentators tend not to focus on the fact that, in fifteen words, we have been given 'three days' journey', 'one day's journey' and 'forty days'. Is this just coincidence and to find a link would be over-reading the text? Or is there an undertone of a passing of time or at least a measuring of time? It would be unwise to take speculative trips (of one or three days) down questionable numerical paths in order to find spurious links, but the reference to the time spans and scales raises questions, nonetheless.

Jonah's message is somewhat ambiguous – 'be overturned/overthrown' may also be translated 'overturn/overthrow itself', which some take to mean 'turn themselves around' – an action the Ninevites took (Trible 1996: 512; Alexander 1988: 121). Stuart (1987: 48) deems: 'There is something of the flavour of the Genesis narratives about Sodom and Gomorrah in this part of the Jonah story', particularly with its use of the words for 'overthrow' and 'violence'.

The Ninevite's response was thorough in terms of the whole population (great and small) and in their actions (fasting and sackcloth) (Jon. 3.5). It was also swift. 'Jonah was just beginning to warm up, just starting the process, and they were already believing God *en masse* (v 5)' (Stuart 1987: 488; see also Trible 1996: 511). In order to explain the reaction of the Ninevites, some have posited the possibility that Jonah might have arrived at the time of a national disaster, such as a famine or flood, or even at a total solar eclipse (e.g. Stuart 1987: 490). One would imagine that the king was the first to be officially informed of events in his city, but by the time he had been told, his people had already responded. Not all have accepted the Ninevites' repentance at face value, however (see Tiemeyer 2022: 187, 199, 246).

Whereas Jonah needed to be told twice to 'arise', the king arises without being told (3.6). Furthermore, he swaps his gown for sackcloth and his throne for sitting in ashes. The proclamation that he sends out is a little dated, for the people are already fasting. The king goes further, however, extending the fast to the animals and precluding drinking (3.7). The animals as well as the humans are to be covered in sackcloth (3.8). How one stops a grazing animal from eating is another issue; presumably, the picture is of muzzled animals. Again, this has generated discussion about whether the animals were led out of the fields into more urban areas. Such suggestions are not necessarily the result of taking the text in an overly literal way, because entering into the world of the text and taking it on its own terms does not mean that one subscribes to the historical nature of it, but it is arguably akin to pushing a metaphor too far to try to ascertain the precise details of such things.

Once they are all showing proper remorse, the king's command is that they cry to God. It is worth noting that the generic word for 'God' is used. The personal name of God (YHWH), is never used in relation to the Ninevites – that is, neither the king nor the narrator use the name of the LORD in ch. 3, perhaps to highlight the Ninevite's non-Israelite status.

While the NIV and NASB put in a word or two to indicate that the humans should cry to God in 3.8, the NRSV follows the Hebrew which says, 'and let them cry to God'. That is, the natural reading of the text is that the animals as well as the humans should cry to God; what is the point of sackcloth and fasting if not? The NRSV also nicely keeps open the second half of the verse with 'All shall turn from their evil ways'. The Hebrew word is 'each' – 'let each turn from his evil way' – and while 'each' is normally used of humans, it is sometimes used of animals, for example, Gen. 7.2 'each/a man with its mate/wife'. At the same time, it is likely that the text is moving in the direction of humans as it talks about 'his evil way and the violence that is in their hands'. As Trible (1994: 185–6) says, however, whether these 'two instructions include the animals remains a moot point.' Bewer (1912: 55) opines that 'a copyist repeated somewhat carelessly *and animals* from v. 7' and that the animals crying to God and repenting, 'was evidently not intended by the original author' though Yael Shemesh (2010: 18) states that 'there is no textual evidence for this proposal and no good reason to accept it'. Ginzberg (2003: 250–1) relates the ancient Jewish myth where 'the Ninevites cried: "If

Thou wilt not have mercy upon us, we will not have mercy upon these beasts,"' which Shemesh (2010: 23) points out is blackmailing God and exploiting his concern for animals.

In another twist of irony, the king's message to the people is far more in keeping with OT prophecy than Jonah's – there is both a call to repentance and an exhortation to leave their evil ways. Significantly, there is also a reference to God. While the king's behaviour is exemplary (if a little extreme) in terms of repentance, one wonders whether the people of his kingdom are slightly ahead of him here as well, for the first thing they do on hearing the message is believe in God. Trible (1996: 513) notes that this is the first time that 'believe' has been used in the story, which takes the Ninevites one step beyond the sailors. The nature of belief is not explored, but is perhaps a more definite response than the king's hopeful, "Who knows? God may turn and be sorry. He might turn from his burning anger and we will not perish" (my translation of 3.9). Jonah knew what the outcome would be (as we see from 4.2), but it seems that he had not passed on the results that repentance would bring. Nevertheless, the king and his people are willing to act 'in faith' in the hope that God would respond to them. They were the model audience of prophecy and their response was what all the OT prophets – apart from Jonah – would have longed for.

The king's words are affirmed by the narrator who repeats them in v. 10 to say that God did relent and they did not perish. While Moberly (1998: 215; see also 2013: 108–11, 120–1) observes that in general the word *shuv* is used for humans repenting, and *niham* is used of God relenting, Gelston (2011: 455) points out that both words are used of God here in Jon. 3.9. The king says that maybe God will turn (*shuv*) and repent (*niham*) and turn away (*shuv*) from his fierce anger. Verse 10 is more in keeping with the general principle: God sees their turning (*shuv*) and relents (*niham*) from the harm that he was to bring them. Gelston (2011: 455) argues that the difference between the words is that *shuv* 'denotes an actual change in attitude, purpose, or action, while [*niham*] focuses rather on the emotional aspect'.

Jonah 4 – plant, worm, wind and sun – and many animals

The start of Jonah 4 seems to be the explanation for Jonah's reluctance to go to Nineveh. A more literal translation of Jon. 4.1 than the English Bibles give would be, 'And it was displeasing/distressing to Jonah – a great displeasure/

distress – and it was hot to him' (my translation). Jonah's reaction is a strong one. Finally, Jonah takes his grievances to the LORD (4.2). As with ch. 2, when Jonah recounts a previous prayer we had not known about, here in ch. 4, he refers to what he had previously said that, again, the story has not narrated till this point. In ch. 1 there is no record that Jonah responds vocally to God's command to go to Nineveh, but here in 4.2 we learn what he apparently had said while he was still in his own country.

Jonah's problem with the LORD was not that he did not understand him, but that he did. Jonah's theology is entirely orthodox and the qualities attributed to God by Jonah in 4.2 were ascribed to God from Moses onwards (Exod. 34.6-7; Num. 14.18; Neh. 9.17, Pss. 86.15, 103.8, 145.8; Joel 2.13; Nah. 1.3). Elizabeth Harper (2002: 462) writes: 'Only Jonah could turn the magnificent creed of Exodus (Ex 34.6, Ps. 86.15, Joel 2.13) into a vindictive denunciation'. Jonah never maligns God, nor misunderstands him; he resists him for who he is. Trible (1996: 481) wryly comments: 'Whereas some prophets shrank from preaching because they saw no hope, Jonah refuses because he knows there is hope.' Even Jonah thought that God's graciousness, mercy, slowness to anger, abundant loving-kindness and propensity to relent in punishing were great when he was the one needing salvation, though Jonah refrains from discussing attributes of God in his psalm of ch. 2 and focuses on the action of being saved. B. K. Smith (1995: 273) stresses: 'The selfishness of this prayer [in 4.2] needs to be noted. The word "I" or "my" [suffixes in Hebrew] occurs no fewer than nine times in the original.'

The sailors had thought that perhaps the LORD would show mercy (1.6) and the Ninevite king had been equally unsure – 'who knows' (1.9), though, arguably, they might have been acknowledging that divine sovereignty involves a freedom for God to act. Jonah, however, had no doubts. He knew and he had known all along that this would be the outcome. This highly predictable ending was why he fled to Tarshish and he makes that quite clear. What Jonah does not explain, however, is why he does not want the Ninevites to be 'forgiven'.

Ginzberg (2003: 251–2) recounts the Jewish legend where Jonah's initial resistance was because he was concerned with God's honour, since God might be made to appear a liar if the Ninevites repented. Some recent commentators have suggested Jonah did not want to be a 'false' prophet by proclaiming a message that did not come to pass (e.g. Limburg 1993: 42), but Perry asks with whom his professional standing would be compromised. 'Surely not the Ninevites, now able to hope, as the result of his warning, for a reversal of the divine decree and for continued life!' (Perry 2006: 54).

As stated in an earlier section, the consensus from Bewer (1912: 57) to Goldingay (2021: 400–1) is that Jonah did not want the Ninevites to experience God's forgiveness because Nineveh, the key city of Assyria, was oppressing Jonah's own people. Joyce Baldwin (1999: 544–5) gives a concise summary of Assyria's harsh treatment of neighbouring countries, including Israel, around this time.

Alexander comments on the irony of Jonah's message saving a people from destruction who are then 'subsequently responsible for the total destruction of his homeland' (1988: 81). Moberly (2013: 200–1) makes a similar point when he refers to the film *Saving Private Ryan*, where the enemy is released with mercy on the proviso that he hands himself in, but instead he goes on to kill those who have shown him mercy. Showing mercy is a risk. Goldingay (2021: 37) suggests that the Jonah story would have been 'more meaningful' to audiences later than Jonah's day, for the Assyrians became a stronger threat. Sherwood (2000: 239) observes that the only other Hebrew prophet called to go to a foreign king was Elisha who was to anoint Hazael king over Syria. Elisha did so with weeping because he knew the brutality with which Hazael would treat his people. Even if Jonah's own people had not suffered under Assyria's brutality at this time, Jonah might have objected to the injustice of forgiveness. Indeed, Goldingay (2021: 400) leans towards it being 'wickedness that offends Jonah'.

It is worth noting, as others have also done, that Jonah does not appear to have a problem with Gentiles per se being delivered, for he is willing to be thrown out of the boat in order that the Gentile sailors do not perish, and even suggests the solution himself. It is Nineveh, in particular, that is the issue. Although we may not be able to discern what was behind Jonah's displeasure, Jonah now has less in common with the prodigal son of Luke 15 and more of the attitude of the older son.

We know that Jonah is angry, but why does he request that God take his life and why is death better than life to him (v. 3)? Perhaps Jonah has lost the battle he has had with God. He does not want this life of being a prophet of God and being forced to utter a message he does not want to utter to a people he does not want to experience God's mercy. God questions Jonah's anger (v. 4), and Alexander (1988: 127) notes the irony that 'having condemned God for not being angry, Jonah is now challenged concerning his own anger'. Jonah does not answer God, however. Instead (v. 5), he leaves the city, makes a shelter for himself from the sun and sits to see what would happen to the city. The king had sat down in repentance, but Jonah's motives for sitting down are quite different.

What did Jonah expect to see? Did he hope that Nineveh might revert to her old ways and that God would overthrow the city after all? Despite his anger – or even because of it – Jonah might simply have wanted to see how things played out. Would Nineveh treat her subjugated people more decently? What would happen when the fasting finished and the sackcloth was put aside? Had such a foreign nation ever behaved in this way before? Jonah was witnessing history, so to speak. Theologically, however, Jonah may be demonstrating that repentance is not the end, but the beginning, of the story.

The LORD God appoints a plant to grow up over Jonah to shade him from the sun, as he had appointed a fish to swallow him. The Hebrew name for the plant is only employed in this place in the Bible and there is no way of knowing what sort of plant it was, any more than it is possible to categorize the fish. That a worm could chew through the stem might suggest a gourd, but other suggestions have been posited. Jonah is exceedingly happy (literally, 'he rejoiced … great joy') about this plant which has grown up very quickly. It is commonly stated that their rate of growth means that you can see bamboo growing and hear rhubarb growing; if this is the case, then one would have been able to see and hear this plant growing! It is another character that is larger than life in the story. At the end of ch. 2 Jonah declared, 'But I, with a voice of thanksgiving, I will sacrifice', but we do not see this 'voice of thanksgiving', even here when there is almost literally an 'in your face' provision from the LORD. It appears that Jonah is still angry with God and his gratitude was short-lived.

Others have often asked why the plant was needed if Jonah had built a shelter for himself. Had the shelter been destroyed? Was it that the shelter was inadequate or only shaded at certain angles? Whatever the reason, it seems that Jonah appreciated the plant for the reason it was given – shade. God asked, 'Are you really *so* upset, Jonah?' (4.3, also v. 9), but Perry (2006: 53) writes:

> His [Jonah's] happiness is so unexpected and exaggerated that we are tempted in turn to ask; 'Are you really *so* happy, Jonah?' For on the face of it, the reaction is absurd: Jonah, the chronically depressed who can take pleasure in nothing, not even in his divine mission, suddenly goes overboard over a plant! Commentators either pass over this absurdity or explain it inadequately.

Perhaps Jonah's emotions are simply another element that are described in exaggerated terms.

The worm appointed by God to attack the plant causes the plant to 'perish' (4.10) and Trible points out that all the characters other than Jonah use 'perish'. That is, the captain declares, 'we will not perish' (1.6), the sailors pray that they won't perish on account of Jonah's life (1.14), the king hopes not to perish (3.9), and God describes the plant as perished (4.10). Jonah is the only one who uses 'die' and 'death' (4.3, 8, 9) (see also Trible 1996: 523).

Until this point, the term 'Lord' has been used by the narrator when telling the story of Jonah himself (as noted, this was not the case when telling the Ninevite story), sometimes on its own and sometimes as 'Lord God'. Jonah himself has used the name of the Lord when he addresses God; where 'God' alone is used in 4.2 it is the generic 'a god'. Here, however, in 4.7, the narrator uses only the general word 'God', which is the form used for the next few verses. Is the narrator indicating that the Lord is stepping back a little in his relationship with Jonah? The narrator uses the term 'the Lord' once again in v. 10, perhaps because Jonah has re-established dialogue with God, albeit a tenuous dialogue. It is ambiguous in v. 8 whether his wish to die is directed to God or himself.

Much has been written about the great fish and the size of whales' stomachs, but little has been written about the size of the worm's stomach who, it would seem, eats like a horse. This worm is on a deadline: it is appointed at dawn, and by the time the sun comes up, it has chewed through enough to bring this plant to its knees, so to speak – a plant large enough to shelter Jonah (Woods 2022: 165). Frethcim (1977: 124) had already exclaimed that the worm caused the plant to dry up 'within minutes!' before Stuart warned that 'any speculation about the exact nature of the gourd, how fast such plants can grow, or the nature of the worm and how fast such worms may eat is useless' (1987: 505). All the non-human characters in the book (some would say, even the boat) are larger than life and also, in contrast to Jonah, go quite some lengths to do God's bidding, though non-human agents probably do not have the choice.

The fish and the plant are appointed for Jonah's benefit, the worm and the sun for his discomfort. As the worm smote the plant, the sun smites Jonah's head and Jonah repeats his wish to die. Whether addressed or not, God answers, and in the same vein as before (4.9). This time, however, rather than questioning Jonah's general anger, he questions Jonah's specific anger over the plant. Jonah's answer rewords God's question and he says that, yes, he has a right to be angry – even to death. Alexander (1988: 130) notes the irony that in v. 3 Jonah was angry with God for delivering, whereas now he is angry for God destroying.

The LORD's response in vv. 10-11 is simple in one sense: Jonah cared about the plant that lasted a day and which he had not tended, so should the LORD not pity Nineveh? In another sense, there is nothing in the text to indicate that Jonah did care about the plant, though Trible challenges this assumption. She notes that the narrator does not give Jonah's reaction to the worm eating the plant, but God fills the gap with his statement about Jonah's pity (Trible 1996: 523–4). Bolin gives a helpful summary of how the word 'pity' can be understood, including, 'sorry to lose' or 'to have concern over' something even if it has no value, for example, Gen. 45.20 (Bolin 1997: 159–62). This gives an easier reading to Jonah's 'pity / compassion for' the plant, but reduces the element of compassion that God has for Nineveh, unless one understands the word in a different way for Jonah and God, which was the initial problem with 'pity'. Is God giving Jonah the benefit of the doubt? If so, then in glossing over Jonah's self-interest, God is living up to the 'graciousness' that Jonah had ascribed to him in 4.2. In so doing, he demonstrates that he has compassion on Jonah as well as the Ninevites. However it should be translated, God, not Jonah has compassion on Nineveh.

Once again, Nineveh is described as 'the great city', yet the ensuing description does not seem to be that of a 'great city'. It is the final reversal in the book of Jonah. The great city is full of highly ignorant people; to be precise, 120,000 people who do not know their right hand from their left. Is 'great' thus used ironically in this final verse of the book? Or is it possible to be both? Or was it great to a compassionate God precisely because it was full of people who could not distinguish one hand from the other? It makes most sense to interpret ignorance in OT terms and equate it with not knowing about God and his ways. Given that the Ninevites acknowledge their evil ways (3.5), it seems that they are quickly becoming less ignorant.

While the book of Jonah is a worked example of Jer. 18.1-10 where God relents because humans repent, the end of the book demonstrates that God's compassion is not a result of seeing Nineveh's repentance, but the cause of sending Jonah to her in the first place – in order that she might repent (see also Trible 1996: 487). The opening verses told us that Jonah had to go to Nineveh because Nineveh's wickedness had come before God (1.2) and now the final verses give us the rest of the reason: because God had compassion on her. Traditionally, the last verse of the book of Jonah (4.11) had been translated as a rhetorical question, though some recent scholars who read against the grain (e.g. Erickson 2021: 406–8) prefer to translate it as a statement, 'I do not have pity on Nineveh … and the animals'. Space prevents a fuller discussion of this, but God shows compassion for animals elsewhere in the OT, for example, the provision of the Sabbath for them (Exod. 20.10, 23.12; Deut. 5.14). As well, if God wanted to express a lack of concern for the Ninevites, why single out their ignorance and not their evil, especially when foreign nations were expected to be ignorant about God? Furthermore, the God presented in the OT would not disregard such abject repentance.

After God's explanation, Jonah never speaks again and we have no record of his reaction. It would be nice to think that the return of the use of 'the LORD' at the end of Jonah 4 adumbrates hope for God's and Jonah's relationship. Bolin (1997: 149) shows that the author of 4.1-11 has crafted the text so that God and Jonah each speak the same number of words, with each speech matched by the other. He argues there is no winner in the dispute (1997: 149), though it should be noted that God has the last word.

The final two words (in Hebrew) of the book of Jonah are arguably a wonderful ending to this quirky book of Jonah. 'And many animals', God says in what is surely a humorous nod to the comically exaggerated scene of Jonah 3. If so, this is a rare insight into God's sense of humour and the closest we get to a wink from God. At the same time, by bringing up the status of the animals so that they are included with humans, the text increases their importance, for they are included as part of the reason why God had compassion on Nineveh. Raising the profile of the animals in a story that treats them with respect, even if there is a humorous element to it, is to do a service to the animal kingdom. Even Calvin acknowledges, 'Oxen were certainly superior to shrubs. If Jonah justly grieved for one withering shrub, it was far more deplorable and cruel for so many innocent animals to perish' (2010 [n.d.]: 144). Stuart (1987: 508) declares: 'The reference to the animals, rather, makes a simple point: God would have every right to spare Nineveh if only because of the dumb animals in it!' Cary (2008: 161) makes the observation that Nineveh abounds in livestock as God abounds in loving-kindness (4.2). It is also a reminder that animal welfare is tightly coupled with human welfare; when God punishes a city and humans struggle economically, the animals will be the first to get hungry tummies. Jonah was told to arise to go to Nineveh partly for the sake of the animals. He tried to run away, but the great fish made sure those Ninevite cows received the blessing that was intended for them!

Concluding reflections on the book of Jonah as Scripture

Jonah is a 'believer', not an 'unbeliever'. Fretheim's assessment is that 'He is a divided man. He will give signs of being a man of faith as well as signs of one who is in theological conflict' (1977: 20). Throughout the OT – and also the NT – there are people who question God's justice. Job's unwarranted suffering probably stands as the most stark example. The book of Jonah is a frank exploration of the tensions between grace, mercy, compassion and forgiveness on the one hand and justice and 'fairness' on the other. In only four chapters, it is easy to see the disparity or the incongruity of the two sides of the coin in a way – even a mildly amusing/ironic way – that readers ancient and modern might miss in their own lives. Jonah implicitly set himself up as the judge of God, but his own sense of justice was rather questionable. While the book of Jonah does have elements of humour, there are still big, serious questions and issues at stake in the book. As Eugene Peterson (1992: 10) claims, 'Some aspects of life and truth can best be explored by means of imaginative play (or playful imagination).' How much readers empathize with the characters in question seems to change over time, according to worldview and no doubt dependent on personality. Jonah has received a range of responses from highly sympathetic to highly critical.

The book of Jonah provides pastoral encouragement to contemporary believers who walk out of line, on occasion. It is not all over for them as it is not for Jonah. That is, Jonah reflects people of faith who need prompting into action, but who do their bit in the end. Peterson reflects:

> We never do get a picture of the kind of pastor we want to be in this story, but only of the kind of pastor we in fact are. Putting the mirror up to us and showing us our double failure would be a severe and unbearable burden if it were not for this other dimension in the story – that God works his purposes through who we actually are, our rash disobedience and our heartless obedience, and generously uses our lives as he finds us to do his work. (1992: 32)

We do not know what happened to Jonah. In a sense, believers themselves may get to write the ending – to fizzle out, spiritually, to stay half-hearted, or to step up to live a life of faithfulness to God, ready to do his bidding. A believing reader who sympathizes with Jonah too much is to side with the one who runs from the presence of God. To look down on Jonah as a failure is to display an attitude arguably similar to that of Jonah himself (cf. Jon. 2.8-9). It is perhaps up to believers in the God of Abraham, Isaac and Jacob to take the ending of the book of Jonah and run with it and give this great story a great ending. It may prompt unbelievers to impress greatly the believers with the great way they live. Regarding the animals, it may encourage humans to live as if 'and many animals' is not a throwaway phrase.

References

Alexander, T. Desmond (1988). 'Jonah: An Introduction and Commentary', in David W. Baker, T. Desmond Alexander and Bruce K. Waltke (eds), *Obadiah, Jonah and Micah*, Tyndale Old Testament Commentaries, 45–131. Leicester: IVP.

al-Ṭabarī, Jarīr (1987). 'Jonah, Son of Amittai', in *The History of al-Tabari, (Ra'rikh al-rusul wa'l-muluk), The Ancient Kingdoms*, vol. 4, ed. Ehsan Yar-Shater, trans. and annotated Moshe Perlmann, 160–6. Albany: State University of New York Press.

Anderson, B. W. (2000). *Out of the Depths: The Psalms Speak for Us Today*, 3rd edn. Louisville, KT: Westminster John Knox Press.

Baldwin, J. (1999). 'Jonah', in Thomas Edward McComiskey (ed.), *The Minor Prophets: An Exegetical and Expository Commentary*, vol. 2. Grand Rapids, MI: Baker.

Bewer, J. A. (1912). 'Jonah', in Hinckley G. Mitchell, John Merlin Powis Smith and Julius A. Bewer (eds), *A Critical and Exegetical Commentary, on Haggai, Zechariah, Malachi, Jonah*, International Critical Commentary on the Holy Scriptures of the Old and New Testaments, 1–65. Edinburgh: T&T Clark.

Bolin, T. M. (1997). *Freedom beyond Forgiveness: The Book of Jonah Re-Examined*, JSOT Supplement Series 236. Sheffield: Sheffield Academic Press.

Calvin, J. (2010 [n.d.]). *Commentaries on the Twelve Minor Prophets*, vol. 3, trans. J. Owen. Logos Bible Software.

Cary, P. (2008). *Jonah*. Grand Rapids, MI: Brazos Press.

Erickson, A. (2021). *Jonah: Introduction and Commentary, Illuminations*. Grand Rapids, MI: Eerdmans.

Fausset, A. R. (n.d.). *A Commentary, Critical, Experimental, and Practical, on the Old and New Testaments: Jeremiah–Malachi*, vol. 4. Glasgow: William Collins, Sons.

Fretheim, T. E. (1977). *The Message of Jonah: A Theological Commentary*. Minneapolis, MN: Ausburg.

Gelston, A. (2011). 'The Repentance of God', in James K. Aitken, Katharine J. Dell, and Brian A. Mastin (eds), *'On Stone and Scroll', Essays in Honour of Graham Ivor Davies*, BZAW 420, 453–62. Berlin: Walter de Gruyter.

Ginzberg, Louis (2003). *From Joshua to Esther*, vol. 4 of *Legends of the Jews*, trans. Henrietta Szold and Paul Radin, 2nd edn. Philadelphia: JPS.

Goldingay, J. (2021). *Hosea–Micah*, Baker Commentary on the Old Testament Prophetic Books. Grand Rapids, MI: Baker.

Habel, N. (1965). 'The Form and Significance of the Call Narratives'. *Zeitschrift für die alttestamentliche Wissenschaft*, 77: 297–323.

Hannah, J. D. (1985). 'Jonah', in J. F. Walvoord and R. B. Zuck (eds), *The Bible Knowledge Commentary: An Exposition of the Scriptures*, vol. 1. Wheaton, IL: Victor Books.

Harper, E. A. (2002). 'Jonah', in Catherine Clark Kroegger and Mary J. Evans (eds), *The IVP Women's Bible Commentary*, 458–63. Downers Grove IL: IVP.

Horne, Charles, and Julius Bewer (1909). *The Bible and Its Story: The Prophets, Isaiah to Ezekiel*, vol. 7. New York: Francis R. Niglutsch (Logos Media Collection).

Hoyt, J. M. (2018). *Amos, Jonah, & Micah*. Lexham Press.

Kadari, Tamar (2016). 'Aggadic Motifs in the Midrash of the Repentance of Jonah the Prophet', in Alberdina Houtman, Tamar Kadari, Marcel Poorthuis, Vered Tohar (eds), *Religious Stories in Transformation: Conflict, Revision and Reception*, Jewish and Christian Perspectives 31, 107–25. Leiden: Brill.

Landes, George M. (1967). 'The "Three Days and Three Nights" Motif in Jonah 2:1'. *Journal of Biblical Literature*, 86 (4): 446–50.

Limburg, J. (1993). *Jonah*, Old Testament Library. London: SCM Press.

Limburg, J. (1988). *Hosea–Micah*. Atlanta, GA: John Knox Press.

Moberly, R. W. L. (1998). 'God Is Not a Human That He should Repent; (Num 23:19 and 1 Sam 15:29)', in Tod Linafelt and Timothy K. Beal (eds), *God in the Fray: A Tribute to Walter Brueggemann*, 112–23. Minneapolis, MN: Fortress.

Moberly, R. W. L. (2003). 'Preaching for a Response? Jonah's Message to the Ninevites Reconsidered'. *Vetus Testamentum*, 53 (Fasc. 2): 156–68.

Moberly, R. W. L. (2013). *Old Testament Theology: Reading the Hebrew Bible as Christian Scripture*. Grand Rapids, MI: Baker Academic.

Nogalski, J. D. (2011). *The Book of the Twelve: Hosea–Malachi*. Macon, GA: Smyth & Helwys.

Nogalski, J. D. (2023). *The Books of Joel, Obadiah, and Jonah*, NICOT. Grand Rapids MI: Eerdmans.

Perry, T. A. (2006). *The Honeymoon Is Over: Jonah's Argument with God.* Peabody, MA: Hendrickson.

Person, R. F. Jr (1996). *In Conversation with Jonah: Conversation Analysis, Literary Criticism, and the Book of Jonah,* JSOT Supplement Series 220. Sheffield: Sheffield Academic Press.

Peterson, E. H. (1992). *Under the Predictable Plant: An Exploration in Vocational Holiness.* Grand Rapids, MI: Eerdmans.

Price, B. F., and E. A. Nida (1993). 'Jonah', in Clark, David J., Norm Mundhenk, Eugene A. Nida and Brynmor F. Price (eds), *A Handbook on The Books of Obadiah, Jonah, and Micah.* New York: UBS.

Shemesh, Yael (2010). '"And Many Beasts" (Jonah 4:11): The Function and Status of Animals in the Book of Jonah'. *Journal of Hebrew Scriptures*, 10. Available online: https://doi.org/10.5508/jhs.2010.v10.a6 (accessed 16 August 2024).

Sherwood, Y. (2000). *A Biblical Text and Its Afterlives: The Survival of Jonah in Western Culture.* Cambridge: Cambridge University Press.

Smith, B. K., and F. S. Page (1995). *Amos, Obadiah, Jonah,* vol. 19B. Nashville, TN: Broadman and Holman.

Stuart, Douglas (1987). *Hosea-Jonah,* Word Biblical Commentary 31. Waco, TX: Word Books.

Tiemeyer, L-S. (2017). 'A New Look at the Biological Sex/Grammatical Gender of Jonah's Fish'. *Vetus Testamentum*, 67 (2): 307–23.

Tiemeyer, L-S. (2022). *Jonah through the Centuries,* Wiley Blackwell Bible Commentaries. Chichester: Wiley-Blackwell.

Torrey, Charles Cutler (1946). *The Lives of the Prophets,* JBL Monograph Series I. Philadelphia, PA: JBL.

Trible, P. (1994). *Rhetorical Criticism: Context, Method, and the Book of Jonah,* Old Testament Series. Minneapolis, MN: Fortress Press.

Trible, Phyllis (1996). 'Jonah', in Leander E. Keck, Thomas G. Long, Bruce C. Birch, Katheryn Pfisterer Darr, William L. Lane, Gail R. O'Day, David L. Petersen, John J. Collins, Jack A. Keller Jr, James Earl Massey, Marrion L. Soards (eds), *Introduction to Apocalyptic Literature, Daniel, The Twelve Prophets,* vol. 7 of *The New Interpreter's Bible: A Commentary in Twelve Volumes,* 461–529. Nashville, TN: Abingdon Press.

Von Rad, G. ([1960] 1975). *Old Testament Theology,* vol. 2, trans. SCM Press. London: SCM Press.

Watts, John D. W. (1975). *The Books of Joel, Obadiah, Jonah, Nahum, Habakkuk, and Zephaniah,* The Cambridge Bible Commentary on the New English Bible. London: Cambridge University Press.

Wiseman, Donald J. (1979). 'Jonah's Nineveh', *Tyndale Bulletin* 30: 29–51.

Wolff, H. W. (1986). *A Continental Commentary: Obadiah and Jonah*. Minneapolis, MN: Augsburg.

Woods, J. I. (2022). 'Furry, Feathery and Fishy Friends – and Insects – in the Book of the Twelve; Their Role and Characterisation', in David G. Firth and Brittany N. Melton (eds), *Reading the Book of the Twelve Minor Prophets*, 151–70. Bellingham, WA: Lexham Academic, 2022.

3

Nahum

Introduction

The book of Nahum is the sermon that Jonah probably would have loved to have preached to Nineveh – as long as its inhabitants did not repent when they heard it. Nahum is infamous for its more uncomfortable aspects. In addition to the traditional elements of an introduction to a biblical book (author, time, place etc.), therefore, in this guide, I will deal seriously with the tone and content of the book of Nahum, and will suggest a new way of reading it.

Nahum and his audience

The book of Nahum describes itself in the first verse as, 'The book of the vision of Nahum the Elkoshite'. This is the only time that Elkosh is mentioned in the OT and its location is unknown, if, indeed, Elkosh denotes a place. Ralph Smith (1984: 63) summarizes a few choices. *The Lives of the Prophets* (an apocryphal work containing stories of OT prophets, written somewhere in the first five centuries CE and possibly originally authored in Greek) identifies Elkosh with Beth-gabre in the land of Simeon which is thought to be the ancient Eleutheropolis and the modern Beit-Jebrin, about twenty miles southwest of Jerusalem. Smith considers that this is the most 'logical' choice. If this is correct, it would put Nahum in the same region as Micah. Other suggestions, however, have identified it with a village about twenty-five miles north of Nineveh, or Capernaum ('the village of Nahum') on the north shore of the Sea of Galilee.

The name 'Nahum' only occurs here in the OT and probably means 'comfort' or 'compassion'. The word for 'vengeance' sounds similar to 'Nahum' and scholars (see Longman III 1993: 766) have noted the wordplay between the two contrasting words, each of which is a theme throughout the book. Nahum is not explicitly described as a prophet, but the fact that he utters oracles (1.1) would imply that he was.

Having addressed Judah in 1.15, the implied audience in 2.1 seems to be Nineveh, which causes an ancient commentator such as Jerome (2016: 14) to comment, parenthetically, 'and this is why the prophets are particularly obscure, because while one thing is happening, the persona is suddenly changed to another.' Indeed, as with the other prophetic books, the implied audience changes and as well as Judah and Nineveh, the onlookers are addressed (3.1-4) and also the King of Assyria (3.18).

Setting Nahum in place and time

Ancient countries did not have designated capital cities in the way that our contemporary world does, but one can think of Nineveh as a/the principal city of Assyria (see the chapter on Jonah for more details). Interestingly, though, while the oracle is to Nineveh (1.1), Nineveh is only mentioned three times by name in the book (1.1, 2.9, 3.7). Ogden (2023: 10) describes the 'marvelous palace' that Sennacherib (704–681 BCE) built; 'its walls decorated with carved relief that illustrated his victory over Lachish. It boasted of gardens and orchards, 80 km. of irrigation that brought water from the mountains to the city. He fortified it with double walls'. Its large library included one account of the Gilgamesh epic, which is the Babylonian Flood story.

Judah, in contrast, was a small nation, completely unable to take on the mighty army of the Assyrian Empire and, to quote Snyman (2020: 36), 'In fact, nowhere in this unit is it even hinted that Judah will act in a military way against Assyria. Judah was in no way a military threat to Assyria, yet it has had to suffer the brutality of the Assyrians.' Nineveh's attackers – the 'mighty men' of 2.3 – are probably Babylon, the empire that followed the Assyrian one.

Assyria, it seems, was particularly cruel, even by ANE standards. While Assyria would have used the terrors of her treatment of prisoners as war propaganda in order to deter nations from attacking her, she boasted of her cruelty. Ashurnasirpal II, who reigned over Assyria from 883–859 BCE claimed:

> I built a pillar over against the city gate and I flayed all the chiefs who had revolted and I covered the pillar with their skins. Some I impaled upon the pillar on stakes and others I bound to stakes round the pillar. I cut the limbs off the officers who had rebelled. Many captives I burned with fire and many I took as living captives. From some I cut off their noses, their ears, and their fingers, of many I put out their eyes. I made one pillar of the living and another of heads and I bound their heads to tree trunks round about the city. Their young men and maidens I consumed with fire. The rest of their warriors I consumed with thirst in the desert of the Euphrates. (Mark 2014: 'Early Reign'; see also O'Brien 2002: 17)

The evidence is still there in the British Museum where, along with the reconstructed gates of Balawat, there are the original bronze panels that graphically portray human heads being used for ornamentation, and humans missing hands and feet, the latter of which can be seen scattered around impaled people. Similar depictions can be seen on wall reliefs in the same museum. It seems as if the unrelenting cruelty of Assyria and one of her main cities, Nineveh, may have been what instigated the prophecy of Nahum.

The reference to the fall of Thebes in Nah. 3.8, which happened in 663 BCE, and the anticipation that Nineveh would fall, which happened in 612 BCE, suggest that the book was set between these dates. If the story of Jonah is set between 790 and 750 BCE (see the chapter on Jonah) and if Nahum's prophecy was shortly before 612 BCE, then Nahum's words are about 150 years later. In this case, Judah would have felt the 'yoke' (Nah. 1.13) of Assyria for more than a hundred years by this point (Watts 1975: 108). Nabopolassar, the king of Babylon, acceded to the throne in 626 at which point he 'took advantage of the Assyrian dynastic troubles to set up a Babylonian state' (Christensen 2009: 62). By the end of 623, his hold on Babylon seems to be secure and in 621 he also had control of Uruk and probably Nippur (Christensen 2009: 62). In 616 he attacked the Assyrians and, in alliance with the Medes, brought the end to Assyria in a war that culminated first with the fall of Asshur in 614 and then Nineveh in 612 BCE (García-Treto 1996: 595). Longman III (1993: 767; see also Ogden 2023: 6) notes that in 1.12 Assyria is 'intact' and with a large population, so Nahum prophesied before Nineveh had begun to crumble. Longman III gives a helpful two-page summary of Assyria's last few years as an empire (1993: 767–8) and Christensen (2009: 52–64) gives a slightly longer, more detailed account of the historical setting of Nahum and Nineveh.

The text of Nahum

Time of writing

Since the book references the fall of Thebes and seems to predate the fall of Nineveh, the book could have been written at the same time as its setting, that is, somewhere between 660 and 612, closer to 612. 'Insofar as the force of the argument depends upon the ability to point to the actual downfall of Nineveh, whether it is imminent or already accomplished, the book must be dated near to 612 B.C.E.' (Sweeney 2000: 425). Secondary arguments scholars utilize, O'Brien explains, include showing that the book cannot have been written after the late Hasmonean period because the Qumran text *Pesher Nahum* references it. Likewise, Josephus cites Nahum in his *Antiquities* (O'Brien 2002: 14). The book references other literature, such as Isaiah, but most scholars are loath to use this to date the whole book because this could be the final redaction of an earlier work, though O'Brien (2002: 15) implies that the reluctance is partly because 'the dating of Nahum to the Assyrian period is well entrenched'. She suggests that this date appeals to scholars because of the wealth of Assyrian material they can draw on in their work, including affirmation that the Assyrians were a cruel nation (O'Brien 2002: 15–18). O'Brien, who is more interested in a 'rhetorical Assyria' rather than a historical one (2002: 22), points out that one of the problems of dating a text due to its contents when its contents are redacted over time is that 'if the entire book is the work of a redactor, then its purpose becomes no longer the prediction of Nineveh's doom by a prophet of the Assyrian period but rather the attempt of a redactor/author to instruct his own community by asking them to consider what an earlier prophet had said about the demise of a well-remembered foe' (O'Brien 2002: 21).

The putative broken acrostic

After Franz Delitzsch's commentary in 1867 in which he accredited Frohnmeyer with discovering at least a partial acrostic in Nahum 1, the first chapter of Nahum attracted attention. Bickell in 1880 reconstructed Nah. 1.2-10 into an acrostic for every letter of the Hebrew alphabet, and Gunkel in 1893 argued for a broken acrostic in 1.1–2.3 which he considered was added by a post-exilic editor (Smith 1984: 65). In 1898, Wellhausen restricted the acrostic to 1.2-8, though Arnold in 1901 considered it spanned 1.1–2.3, some of which he attributed to a late fourth-century redactor. Paul Haupt in 1907 deemed that Nahum was not prophecy, but liturgy, and the last part of the acrostic was not used because it did not suit the liturgical purpose. Humbert (1926) limited the acrostic to 1.2-8 and saw Nahum as prophetic liturgy. Ralph Smith's tightly packed summary (1984: 65–6) of Nahum's broken acrostic has formed the basis of this paragraph. While most scholars accept the broken acrostic in some form or another (e.g. Achtemeier 1986: 6; Longman III 1993: 769; García-Treto 1996: 596; Snyman 2020: 20), some such as O'Brien (following Floyd's 1994 work) doubt its existence, not least because of the number of emendations and literary acrobatics needed to make it work (O'Brien 2002: 47; see also Sweeney 2000: 427; Ogden 2023: 16). In the main, however, it is no longer a burning issue, and Renz (2021: 28) is probably representative in tone when he says, 'If an alphabetic acrostic underlies the poem, its likely end point is in v. 7 or 8.'

Transmission and redaction

Christensen (2009: 64) states, 'The Hebrew text within the Masoretic tradition has been transmitted with great care and relatively little evidence of textual corruption.' Christensen's view is that scholars used to suggest many emendations (see the footnotes to the Biblia Hebraica Stuttgartensia – BHS), but following Spronk (1997) who re-evaluated the issues and suggested few alterations, 'an increasing number of scholars today share similar beliefs' (Christensen 2009: 65). The LXX (the Greek translation called the Septuagint) and the MT differ in a number of places, but Christensen affirms that these are translator errors or misunderstandings rather than there being a different Hebrew version underlying the LXX. Other Greek versions, namely those of Aquila, Symmachus and Theodotion are closer to the MT (Christensen 2009: 64).

While textual corruptions may be few, redactions appear to be many. Renz (2021: 42–3) explains that when a text is disjointed, scholars suspect redaction and while, historically, changes of pronouns, gender and number have been seen as disjoints, now these are accepted as possible Hebrew style.

In Nahum, however, these sorts of changes, 'seem to go together with generic differences'. (43). O'Brien (2002: 21) notes that, 'the book's translational difficulties … are often credited to less-than-judicious editing'.

Genres

OANs as oracles or burdens

The book of Nahum opens with, 'The oracle of Nineveh. The book of the vision of Nahum the Elkoshite'. Oracles against the nations (OANs) occur in all three of the major prophetic books: Isaiah 13–23; Jeremiah 46–51; and Ezekiel 25–32 and in more than half the books of the Minor Prophets/Book of the Twelve if one counts Jonah (Joel, Amos, Obadiah, Jonah, Nahum, Zephaniah and Zechariah). The terms 'nations' and 'foreign nations' mean nations other than Israel and Judah. The books of Obadiah and Nahum are entirely concerned with prophesying against, respectively, Edom and Nineveh.

The word used for 'oracle' or 'burden' comes from the verb 'to lift up' and is commonly used at the start of OANs. It might mean that the heavy words were a load upon the prophet who pronounced them. Alternatively, they might be heavy weights which must be lifted up and borne by the people to whom the words were announced. It is perhaps only a small change in nuance to see the OANs as burdens concerning the nations rather than oracles against them, but one that allows for empathy. This terminology or 'burden' in relation to the OANs is particularly prevalent in Isaiah – see Isa. 13.1 re Babylon; 14.28 re Philistia; 15.1 re Moab; 17.1 re Damascus; 19.1 re Egypt; 21.1 re the wilderness of the sea – Babylon; 21.11 re Edom; 21.13 re Arabia; 22.1 re valley of vision; 23.1 re Tyre; and 30.6 re the beasts of the Negev; see also Zech. 9.1 re Hadrach – Damascus. At the same time, 'burden' may be employed for oracles against Israel and Judah as well as individuals, and both Habakkuk and Malachi begin with the word in a national context (see also 2 Kgs 9.25; Jer. 23.33, 34; Ezek. 12.10; Zech. 12.1; 2 Chron. 24.27). The book of Nahum is following common practice, then, in beginning with this word, especially as an oracle/burden against/concerning Nineveh (a foreign city) then follows. It should be noted that the term 'oracles against/concerning the nations' is not a biblical term, but a scholarly one. While both 'oracle/burden' and 'vision' are common ways for prophecies to begin, Nahum is distinct in the phrase, 'the book of the vision', for this phrase is nowhere else used in the Bible and no other prophetic book even starts by describing itself as a 'book'.

Visions and word

Prophetic books often refer to their content as 'visions', which may seem a bit confusing given that they consist of speeches. The word 'vision' can also conjure up an image of a mystical, exotic and sensational experience; one might think of Ezekiel's and Isaiah's heavenly visions and Daniel's apocalyptic ones. The biblical use is usually far less glamorous in the main, however, and a crude understanding of 'vision' in the prophetic literature is often simply a picture of what the future looks like as things stand right now. That is, the prophet envisions a future of God's punishment if the people continue behaving wickedly. This idea of a 'vision' is demonstrated by passages such as Ezek. 7.13 where the vision will not be averted, or in Ezek. 12.27 where the vision the prophet sees is for many days from now. In this sense, 'visions' have more to do with wisdom and discernment in terms of being able to see or forecast future consequences of current behaviour than they have to do with dramatic dream experiences. Even Daniel, whose visions are more sensational, is credited with having knowledge, intelligence and insight to understand literature, wisdom, visions and dreams (Dan. 1.17).

That is not to say that OT prophetic visions are simply common-sensical forecasts which are devoid of God, for God gives visions in the OT (Ps. 89.19; Hos. 12.10), as he gives wisdom to those who stand in his counsel. Jeremiah makes clear that the difference between a true and a false prophet is that false prophets 'speak a vision of their hearts' (Jer. 23.16, my translation) rather than of God's heart. That is, false prophets tend to paint a picture of well-being irrespective of people's behaviour (Jer. 14.14-15; see also Ezek. 12.24, 13.16). A false vision is thus a picture where repentance is not necessary. True prophets hope that the vision will shake the people into responding to God when they see their bleak future sketched out. A modern analogy might be that climate experts give a vision of the future if people do not change their energy consumption and carbon footprint and the like. The ideal response is that the predicted image does not become reality but is averted by a change for the better.

Prophetic visions are not distinct from the prophetic word and in many cases intrinsically linked to it as others have noted – see Longman III's (1993: 769–70) brief paragraph-long excursus. They may be explicitly spoken, for example, 'they are prophesying to you a false vision' (Jer. 14.14, see also Jer. 23.16), twinned with the words of the LORD, for example, 'word from the LORD was rare in those days, visions were infrequent' (1 Sam. 3.1; see also Ezek. 12.27, 13.16; Hos. 12.10; 1 Chron. 17.15; 2 Chron. 32.32), or implicitly linked when an oracle of prophecy follows a vision, for example, 'The vision of Obadiah. Thus says the Lord GOD …' (Obadiah 1; see also Isa. 1.1).

While prophetic visions and utterances go hand in hand, in some places visions are linked to the law. Prov. 29.18; Lam. 2.9; Ezek. 7.26 are such examples. The surrounding verses in Proverbs 29 are to do with correction and keeping people in the right way, so Prov. 29.18 continues that thought; 'Where there is no vision, the people are unrestrained, But happy is he who keeps the law.' The implication is that the vision is the correcting force. This is a main purpose of prophecy, and thus appropriate that vision and prophecy are sometimes combined. Both Lam. 2.9 and Ezek. 7.26 bemoan the lack of law and prophetic vision in times of punishment, paying tribute to the fact that the correcting force has been absent.

A number of prophetic books other than Nahum open with an explanation that it is a vision or something the prophet saw ('saw' and 'vision' having the same root in Hebrew): Isaiah ('visions' which he 'saw'), Amos ('saw'), Obadiah ('vision'), Micah ('saw') and Habakkuk ('saw'). Although Ezekiel saw visions, different root words underlie 'saw' and 'vision', which is fitting given the nature of his visions, which are more dramatic, ecstatic experiences than the majority of visions described above.

Nahum is a short book, so its self-description as a 'book' might be surprising. Watts (1975: 100), however, remarks, 'The word [normally translated 'book'] can refer to a written text of any size.' In fact, the word is used in Deut. 24.1 for a 'certificate' of divorce. Even so, the opening description of the book of Nahum as burden, book and vision is weighty for such a short work. One cannot read too much into this, but it is in keeping with Nahum's bold and stark prophecy. Nahum speaks in 'capital letters', as we might say in English.

The genre of acrostic poems

Nahum's so-called broken acrostic extols God's more fearsome characteristics. García-Treto (1996: 601), drawing on Alter (1985: 146–7), comments that acrostic poems in the OT are intended for liturgy, and when prophecy uses such a liturgical form, it is sometimes in order to move something from a particular historical context to an 'archetypal horizon' (Alter's phrase, 146) 'whose outer limit is myth'. Alter argues (García-Treto does not cite him on this):

> For all that has been written about the demythologizing impulse of the Hebrew Bible, prophetic poetry exhibits a certain predilection to mythologize its historical subjects, setting the here and now in cosmic perspectives. This happens most often in the monitory poetry of impending disaster, where warnings about concrete threats to the land and its people easily shade into the vaster terrors of apocalyptic vision. (Alter 1985: 147)

García-Treto sees Nah. 1.2-8 as an example of this:

> The events relating to the impending fall of the Assyrian Empire are aligned against the "archetypal horizon" of the basic ancient Near Eastern myth of the divine warrior, emerging to do battle against his enemies. These enemies are identified, at times, with the forces of chaos that threaten the order of creation, with death-dealing drought, or with human adversaries who threaten the nation. (García-Treto 1996: 601)

If this is the case, then it is another hermeneutical constraint against reading prophecy in a 'literalistic' or 'wooden' way, particularly prophecy such as the book of Nahum.

Woe oracles

Nahum 3 starts with a brief 'woe' oracle. Woe oracles have their origins in funeral laments, but the prophets often use them rhetorically and a woe oracle uttered over the living as if they were dead indicates that the punishment is irrevocable. García-Treto (1996: 613) states that the verse is a 'performative speech that vents anger'. There are two Hebrew words that begin woe oracles and Nahum has the 'softer' form, which is often translated 'Ah' rather than 'Woe'. There is also no 'to' in the Hebrew text that follows, so while the NIV and NASB have 'Woe to …', the NRSV more faithfully renders the Hebrew with 'Ah! City of bloodshed …'. The question of tone is always a key hermeneutical question to ask of any text, but there is good reason to read the tone here (and arguably in other prophetic woe oracles) as one of regret.

Nahum's poetry

Prophetic visions are often highly metaphorical and paint stark and frightening pictures and the 'book of the vision of Nahum' probably leads the way in terms of its extreme depictions and troubling metaphors. One example of the vivid depictions is the way that the warriors are dressed in scarlet, brandishing red shields, and the chariots rush madly and wildly, like torches or lightning flashes (Nah. 2). The whole scene is fiery, and the chapter ends with God burning Nineveh's chariots in smoke (v. 13). This is what it looks like when God's way is the whirlwind and the storm (using words from 1.3). Examples of the stark metaphors include the strong lions reduced to moaning like the sound of doves (v. 7), or the charming prostitute who lures nations only to sell them (3.4), or the familiar metaphor of locust swarms (3.15-17). Less stark, but persistent, is the imagery of water that runs throughout Nahum (1.4, 8; 2.8; 3.6, 8, 14). Despite its content, many (e.g. Achtemeier 1986: 5; Longman III 1993: 771–2; O'Brien 2002: 65) have commented on the fine poetry in the book of Nahum.

If Nahum had used paints rather than words, he might have used brightly coloured oils, plastered on thickly with a palette knife, or the lines would be sharp and distinct and the shapes tending towards the grotesque. Nahum's painting would be one that caught the eyes of visitors entering the art gallery, even if it did not hold their hearts. Indeed, many would recoil in distaste – as, indeed, they should. Readers and hearers of prophecy are not expected to listen and 'enjoy' the picture painted any more than its original recipients were. The picture is supposed to elicit horror, disgust and communal self-reflection that asks, 'Is this what you want?', a theological point which will be developed over the next few pages. To have a picture that one can live with and hang in the best room of the house would be missing the point. People would not change their lives for such a picture, though, of course, there are visions of hope and future restoration in prophecy. It is important to remember when interpreting Nahum that prophecies/visions are an artistic representation of a possible future, not an actual one and it is a future that can be averted. In the case of the book of Nahum, that artistic representation of Nineveh's future is crude and violent at times, but it is picture language.

Nahum 1 – God's nature and responsibilities

Nahum's vision-prophecy begins with what is often described as a hymn to the Divine Warrior. It opens with a declaration that the Lord is a jealous God and avenging on his enemies (1.2). In all the other instances where this adjectival form of 'jealous' is used, it is in the context of Israel's covenant and his people not worshipping other gods (Exod. 20.5, 34.14; Deut. 4.24, 5.9, 6.15; Josh. 24.19; 1 Kgs 19.10, 14). God is described as a jealous God in the above passages, other than in 1 Kings where it is Elijah who is jealous/zealous for God. Given that foreign nations were not expected to worship Israel's God, it is perhaps surprising to find the word used in this oracle against Nineveh until one realizes that Nahum is giving God's side of the covenant and his responsibilities. God's being jealous is twinned with him being avenging and it is likely that he is jealous over his people Israel and will avenge them for wrongs done to them. The phrase, 'the LORD is avenging' is used three times in this verse. When Hebrew repeats itself, then it is making a point. The book of Nahum's vision is a picture of what Israel's God looks like when he is avenging her. It also makes plain that God is not acting arbitrarily against the Ninevites on a whim but is punishing for a reason – vengeance.

God's self-description in Exod. 34.6, 'The LORD, the LORD God, compassionate and gracious, slow to anger, and abounding in lovingkindness and truth …' becomes a creedal statement quoted frequently in the Bible – see Num. 14.18; Neh. 9.17; Ps. 86.15, 145.8; Joel 2.13; Jon. 4.2; and Nah. 1.2. O'Brien (2022: 48) displays Exod. 34.6 and Nah. 1.2 in parallel and notes that 'the structure of Nah. 1.2 clearly prioritizes the LORD's vengeance'. Indeed, it is interesting that both prophets concerned with Nineveh – Jonah and Nahum – 'misuse' this verse from Exodus. Jonah is angered by God's merciful nature and uses the verse against God while Nahum emphasizes God's vengeance and wrath (words that are not used in Exod. 34.6). Furthermore, God's words in Exod. 34.6 were in the context of the covenant with his people and his punishment was to be upon his own people, whereas Nahum presents God's vengeance and wrath as being against his enemies (see also O'Brien 2002: 49).

The next verse (1.3) pays tribute to God's slowness to anger and then there is another declaration that God will punish. The NRSV and NIV, among other translations, translate the conjunction *waw* as 'but' which is fitting, that is, 'The LORD is slow to anger, but great in power' (NRSV, NIV). The LORD's slowness to anger does not mean that he will not punish. This is both a comfort to those who have felt Nineveh's continual evil and a warning to those who might be complacent about God's slowness to anger.

The rest of v. 3 and the next few verses pay tribute to God's power over the natural world, particularly his destructive power. In contrast to Elijah who experienced God as a 'still small voice' or 'gentle blowing/whisper', even 'silence' (1 Kgs 19.12), here in Nahum, God's way is in the whirlwind and storm. Verse 6 makes the point, by way of rhetorical questions, that no one can stand up against the God who has such power over the earth and heavens. Some scholars (e.g. Ralph Smith 1984: 74; García-Treto 1996: 602) view the references to the sea and the rivers in the first line of v. 4 as drawing on Canaanite mythology and shows as well that the Lord can do what Baal cannot (Ralph Smith 1984: 74). This may be so, but it is also language used in theophanies when the earth, weather and even the cosmos are churned up at or alongside God's appearance (even if theophanic language is rooted in Canaanite myth). How much v. 6 refers to river waters flooding the area causing the foundations of the buildings to be compromised, leading to their collapse, and how much is simply metaphorical language in a poem is debated. Watts (1975: 113), for instance, says, of the 'supernatural' level of the text that '*the rivers* are the currents of the great cosmic ocean' which are generally thought of as destructive (cf. the flood in Genesis 7) and which had to be pushed back at creation. For more on the theme of water in Nahum, see William Briggs' 2018 paper, 'The Interplay of Water and Gender in Nahum'.

Verses 7 and 8 reiterate that while the Lord is good and a refuge for those who trust him, his enemies will not escape. Again, translating the *waw* beginning v. 8 as 'but' (NASB and NIV) highlights the contrast: God is good to those who take refuge in him, but he will punish his enemies (Achtemeier 1986: 9–10; Ralph Smith 1984: 76). In other words, a person's/nation's experience of God is dependent on whether they trust him or set themselves up against him. Given this knowledge, v. 9 asks why the addressee would set itself up against him. Going against God is a pointless exercise because it will fail, or to use the words of 1.9, 'Whatever you [plural] devise against the Lord, He will make a complete end of it.' This is the first time that the second person is used and as yet we do not know who the addressees are (García-Treto 1996: 604). Given the prologue, we would expect it to be Nineveh and most see v. 11 as referring to Nineveh – see Christensen's overview of the options (2009: 231–2). Verse 12 begins a new utterance ('Thus says the Lord') and it seems that God is addressing his people in vv. 12-13 before turning his attention to Nineveh in v. 14 (Christensen 2009: 247). Perhaps these verses are deliberately ambiguous with regard to the audience, or are intended for the most part to be general statements about God which does not necessitate any specific audience. It is worth noting that Nah. 1.10 is notoriously difficult to translate – see the commentaries (e.g. Ralph Smith 1984: 76; Christensen 2009: 208; Renz 2021: 84–6).

Verses 12-14 explain that God has afflicted his people (possibly because of their plotting against the LORD if they, rather than Nineveh, are the addressees in v. 11). The agent of his affliction is implicit and, given the context, is Nineveh: 'I will break his [Nineveh's] yoke bar from upon you' (v. 13). Isaiah also uses this language when talking about casting off the Assyrian yoke (10.27, 14.25 – see also Isa. 9.4 where Assyria is again implicitly understood, though not named). In fact, Nahum is reminiscent in other places of Isaiah, for example, v. 15 (Nah. 2.1 in the Hebrew), which nicely follows on from v. 13 in continuing to announce good news, and employs the same language as Isa. 52.7, though Renz (2021: 106–9) concludes that the allusion does not affect the interpretation of Nahum. Coggins looks at other resonances with Isaiah in his short commentary on Nahum (1985: 5–63). Verse 15 continues by encouraging Judah to celebrate, 'For never again will the wicked one pass through you.'

Verse 14 seems somewhat out of place between these two verses of hope because it is an oracle of judgement against his people in which God says that he will cut off their idols and images, and prepare their grave, 'For you are contemptible'. Most English translations have something akin to 'The LORD has issued a command concerning you' (v. 14) where the 'you' is usually thought to refer to the king of Assyria, due to the context and perhaps reference to 'the house of your [masculine singular] gods' (García-Treto 1996: 605).

Nahum 2 – revenge is sweet! Or is it?

Nahum 2 begins with a battle cry summoning Nineveh (the implied 'you') to summon her strength because God is restoring the splendour (literally 'pride' which usually has negative overtones) of Jacob, despite her being devastated. In this, we see the avenging God of ch. 1 going into battle on behalf of his people; Nineveh is going to experience some of what she inflicted on others.

God remembers Nineveh's 'nobles' (NASB) or 'officers' (NRSV) in 2.5 who hurry to the city walls in order to escape, only to find that the city is under siege and they are trapped in a closed city while the gates of the river are wide open and flooding the palace (v. 6). This verse (v. 6) and v. 8 are ironic because Nineveh had been like a pool of water (v. 8) and now the burst river has 'dissolved' her palace. While NASB and AV's translation is 'dissolved' and ESV's is 'melts', the NRSV's 'trembles' and NIV's 'collapses' are less literal renderings.

Nineveh's people flee and ignore calls to stop (v. 8), which leaves the city and her limitless treasures open to plunder (v. 9). As with most biblical texts, there are various issues of translation in Nahum, which good commentaries cover, but it is worth noting that v. 7 is another verse that is extremely difficult to translate, particularly the first three words. Christensen (2009: 287–91) gives an excellent summary of the issues with the various translational options.

By Nah. 2.10, the picture that Nahum presents is that of a desolate wasteland devoid of people and stripped of everything of worth. Those who remain, or perhaps those who are fleeing – the Ninevites, in either case – are in abject fear (v. 10) so that vv. 11-12 read as a mocking taunt; what has happened to this fearless people who preyed on others like lions and terrorized them?! The chapter ends with God declaring that he is against Nineveh which reiterates that it is God who is behind their destruction. The Ninevites had seen themselves, metaphorically, as the top of the food chain, but there was one who was stronger than they, who could take out even the strongest of these young lions (v. 13). Moreover, he would cut off their prey, that is, he would rescue those they had formerly terrorized. Gordon Johnston (2001, 287–307) has written an insightful paper about the double use of the lion motif in the book of Nahum in terms of the lion hunt and the royal-lion metaphor, both of which were popular in Assyrian royal culture.

O'Brien (2002: 65) writes of 2.2-13, 'The sounds of the Other's terror are made appealing to the ear, to the senses. Built in to the very craft of the book is delight in – or at least fascination with – another's suffering.' She argues that the effects of such pleasure is to destabilize reading. I would agree that the start of ch. 2 is to engage and even excite the reader with the military scene, but disagree that Nahum's poetry is intended to lead to delight or necessarily even fascination with another's suffering. Rather, I would argue that the poetry is intended to lead – without comment – from the excitement of an imminent battle to the horror and discomfort in the chaos and brutality of war and the suffering of others. At whichever point the reader 'stumbles in their march' (Nah. 2.5) will depend on the reader but, at some point, those who are geared up for battle at the start of ch. 2 and looking for vengeance on the enemy are likely to adjust their position as they continue reading Nahum. For now, though, Nahum's poetry continues into ch. 3 where the redness of the picture continues, though this time blood red.

Nahum 3 – Nineveh broken beyond repair

Nahum 3 is the most troubling chapter in the book of Nahum with its brutal imagery, including that of a humiliated woman. The brief 'woe' oracle that starts the chapter (see section on 'Genres') reminds the hearer/reader that Nineveh is a terrorizing power that continually runs with the blood of her victims. In addition, not only is the city cruel but also corrupt in terms of deception and plundered goods. The bloody city will now run with her own blood. The poetry of vv. 1-3 is possibly the best in the book of Nahum. 'The use of short couplets (and one triplet) adds emotion and vividness to the battle scene' (Christensen 2009: 348). Indeed, it conjures up well the frenetic battle scene, and the visual and auditory details grab the attention of the eyes and ears of the one witnessing it. The fixation on the dead bodies at the end is a horror from which the observer cannot seem to avert their eyes. It is undoubtedly verses like this which lead O'Brien (2002: 65; see above) to conclude that there is delight in another's suffering. A better nuance might be to see it as shock, perhaps even morbid curiosity ('fascination', to use O'Brien's own word), a common human trait, but one which leads to nightmares, not pleasure. In fact, any confident triumph in God's absolute vengeance with which the book arguably begins has surely faded somewhat by this point in the text; there are more layers to Nahum's book of vision than appear at first glance.

Shaming or rape

The language of harlotry and sorcery (v. 4) portrays the deep feelings of the author/Nahum/God about the damage that Nineveh has done to other nations – enslaving them and filling her streets with their blood. The prostitute imagery (which is a common trope in the prophetic literature) continues into the next verse (v. 5) where the metaphor is used against Nineveh. This is not a reversal, as such, because Nineveh does not experience what she has done to others. It is more that Nineveh is being exposed for what she is, and shamed. She has lured others with her charm and sorceries, implying deceit, but those nations who were seduced will no longer see the charm but the naked truth. In terms of the text's prostitute imagery, Nineveh's nakedness is no longer on her terms and in being exposed, she is shamed and disgraced. The LXX's sense is 'I shall uncover your buttocks in your presence' (Christensen's translation – 2009: 344).

The passage presents the prostitute as the 'abuser' (to use anachronistic language) who is exposed, rather than as the 'abused', and Thomas Renz (2021: 57) argues:

> We are not to think of a woman driven to prostitution to make a living. Nineveh is not the victim of a system that forces her to sell her body to make ends meet. She is a source of ensnarement and ready to sell peoples for her pleasure ... This distances the metaphor from "ordinary" prostitution and suggests that the text is not intended to be read as saying something about prostitutes or women in general.

Others, nevertheless, have extrapolated in this way and also extrapolated the shaming to be rape. Magdalene (2004: 327), for instance, draws attention to verses that include Nah. 3.5 (as well as 2.6-7 and 3.13):

> Within these verses, God, characterized as male, is regularly threatening, in judgement, to rape, or otherwise sexually abuse, the cities of Israel, Judah and their neighbors, all characterized as a female. Metaphorically, then, God is seemingly quite willing to perpetrate repeated sexual assaults and abuse on women. Such texts are the ultimate in biblical texts of terror. Not only is God a passive participant in the sexual assaults on and abuse of women in the narrative portions of the Hebrew Bible by his lack of intervention on behalf of the raped and abused, God is an active perpetrator of such sexual violence against women in the prophetic corpus of the Bible.

See also O'Brien (2002: 28, 73, 87, 91, 93, 94, 95 × 3, 96, 97, 98 × 2 etc.) for similar comments on rape in Nahum. There are problems in seeing Nah. 3.5 as rape, however, including needing to broaden the definition of what is commonly understood as rape, and to read the text as implying more than it explicitly states (in a text that does not shy away from depicting horror). To Renz's observations about the metaphor not featuring a 'normal' prostitute, one could add that the prostitute in this metaphor is one who sheds blood. It is an ugly metaphor but, like many metaphors, cannot be pressed too far in terms of literal comparisons – compare with the lions of 2.12 who fill their lairs with prey when lions do not live in lairs or dens and generally also eat their prey where they kill it. There is a fear among some interpreters that other less enlightened people will read texts such as Nah. 3.5 as encouraging men to rape women. Carol Dempsey (2021: 96) warns: 'The evangelical fundamentalist approach to reading the Bible adopted by the evangelical Christian right and the Catholic right turns the Minor Prophets' biblical metaphors into biblical literalism so that the metaphors point the way to how people, especially males, should act literally.' This unsourced statement would be offensive to many/most among those she has named and shamed.

The author of Nahum realizes that such stripping is deeply shameful for a woman and is a horrifying act. As Gregory Cook (2016: 345) points out, 'a close reading of 3:4–7 shows that YHWH strips the queen in order to remove her erotic attraction – not to exploit it'. To say that our sensibilities are not those of the ANE is not to 'hide behind the text' but needs to be acknowledged. At the same time, while the biblical authors might not have had our sensibilities, neither did they peddle such images as pornography intended for sexual gratification, something that is rife (with worse images than found in the book of Nahum) in our contemporary world. Nineveh had been charming and alluring ('sexual predator' might carry a better sense to modern ears than 'prostitute'), now she is shamed and made a vile spectacle from which others shrink and the image is intended to repel (v. 7).

Watts (1975: 116) surmises that the prostitute imagery was probably used because Ishtar (Nineveh's 'patroness') was the goddess of sex and war and 'her temples were furnished with sacred prostitutes' (Watts 1975: 116). Given Nineveh's military success, Ishtar's reputation would have been good, but when Nineveh fell, her gods, including Ishtar, fell with her. According to Watts (1975: 116),

> She [Ishtar] was even called a harlot in descriptions by some of her worshippers. Stories of her exploits included acts of savagery and destruction. She was a most fitting symbol for the brutal empire. With lustful visions of riches and power Ishtar had *beguiled nations* into war and conquest. Like the Devil of Christian thought, she tempted and demonized all who came within her influence.

Watts does not reference his sources, but they are likely to be *A hymn to Inana as Ninegala (Inana D)* and *A šir-namšub to Inana (Inana I)*. *Inana D* praises Inana (the Sumerian name of the Babylonian Ishtar): 'They cannot compete with you, Inana. As a prostitute you go down to the tavern' (lines 95–106) and 'The pearls of a prostitute are placed around your neck,' (lines 109–15) while in *A šir-namšub to Inana (Inana I)*, Inana/Ishtar says of herself, 'I am a prostitute familiar with the penis' (lines 16–22). Watt concludes his short commentary on Nahum by warning the reader to keep the perspective of the book: Nineveh and Assyrian are not 'ordinary' oppressors, but 'stand for the ultimate supernatural evil that frustrates and suppresses the purposes and people of God' (120).

At the same time, Nahum is self-subversive. That is, while this vision of Nahum's of the vengeance of God for his people provides a voice for them (the implied audience when it was written and the real audience of today), it also arguably intends to unsettle and disturb. By so doing, it raises the question about what it means to call for God's vengeance and how much they actually want God to exact.

Detested things

In 3.6, God threatens to throw 'detested things' on Nineveh in the continued metaphor of her as a prostitute. The Hebrew word here in Nah. 3.6 – 'detestable things' – is often used for idols or even food. If the detestable things are, in fact, idols then it is probably to continue to highlight what Nineveh is in an unvarnished way: an unveiling that shows a contemptible image far from desirable. The LXX translates it with a word that means 'abomination' as does Maier (1980: 7). Most English versions translate the word as 'filth' (e.g. NRSV, NASB, NIV, ESV, NJB, GNB, 'abominable filth' AV), which is perhaps unfortunate given the modern reader's association with filth as excrement. Indeed, some have taken that sense, including *The Message*, which is a paraphrase of the Bible and thus translates rather freely, 'dog dung'. While Christensen (2009: 344) says that 'it is possible that the word … carries the connotation of "excrement"', there is nothing in the Hebrew to suggest that it was excrement. Indeed, there are a number of Hebrew words for 'excrement', 'human waste' or 'dung', that could have been utilized, such as that found in Deut. 23.13 and Ezek 4.12, or that used in 2 Kgs 6.25, 18.27, or the one employed in Job 20.7. Longman III (1993: 817) writes, 'It is a rare word, which Rashi mistook to mean "excrement", a translation that the NEB accepts' and, indeed, perhaps others have followed Rashi. John Smith considers that translating the word as 'idols' 'seems forced' ([1911] 1965: 339) and that 'filth' better fits the context of a woman being shamed. It is possible that other similar translations are also a result of the imagined scene. While some of the commentaries suggest the better translations of 'detested things' or 'any loathsome object on which they can lay hand' (Maier [1959] 1980: 309) and such like, some use unwarranted emotive language, such as Ralph Smith's 'She will be defiled with abominable filth (v. 5) [sic]' (1984: 86) which uses two different variations of the word – 'abomination' and 'filth' – and puts them together to make a stronger and more evocative meaning than is in the text itself. Calvin (2005: 488) does likewise. More wisely and less emotively, Clark and Hatton (1989: 46) suggest to those translating Nahum into 'minority languages' that they might like to use 'rubbish' given that 'all sorts of household rubbish' was probably intended. The 1917 JPS TANAK version has 'detestable things' and JPS's more recent (1985) version has 'loathsome things'. García-Treto (1996: 614) considers that the phrase is an idiom that can mean, 'I will defame you.'

Verse 6 continues with, 'I will treat you with contempt' (as with NRSV, NIV and ESV, but against NASB and AV's 'make you/thee vile') and ends with, 'I will make you a spectacle' as most of the more reliable English translations have it. Thus the more literal translation of v. 6 is 'I will throw detestable things upon you, And treat you with contempt, And make you a spectacle'. In fact, all who see her will flee from her (v. 7), no longer taken in by her lies (v. 1) and her charm (v. 4).

Quotation marks and speaker

There will be a recognition that Nineveh is destroyed (v. 7), but, as Clark and Hatton (1989: 47) comment, 'The main problem in this verse is to decide where the quotation ends.' As the leading English translations have it, the same onlookers who comment on Nineveh's destruction are those who then ask, 'Who will grieve for her?', with the following question coming from the prophet/God; 'Where will I seek comforters for you?' This short rhetorical question, from those who see her, succinctly sums up the prevailing attitude for the predator city and we are reminded of the last words of the book, 'For on whom has not your evil passed continually?' At the same time, with all that has gone before, is the question quite as rhetorical as it seems? Those who have suffered under Nineveh's brutality and cruelty and who may have been praying psalm-like prayers for God's vengeance might not, at this point, be quite as certain as they were that they would not bemoan the city's fall, given the piles of dead humans that a city's fall entails. Perhaps the question belongs, after all, on the lips of the narrator. In any case, there are (at least) two ways of reading it: the question asked by the onlookers; and the question asked by the enduring text (if not the implied author) to its audience.

No-amon and a reading strategy for Nahum

Verses 8-10 ask, rhetorically, if Nineveh thought she was better than No-amon (Thebes), one of the most important Egyptian cities which, despite having allies, was overthrown by Assyria in about 663 BCE (Grayson 2008: 144). John Smith ([1911] 1965: 342) advises, that 'allowance must be made for the fact that Nahum had almost certainly never seen Thebes and consequently was dependent for his information upon the reports of merchants and travellers'. The mention of the children dashed to pieces (v. 10) along with the honourable men for whom lots were cast (v. 10), suggest that a sympathetic response is intended. Once again, as they did by using 'filth' over 'detestable things' in v. 6, the English versions tend towards a more emotive and sensational translation of 'small/young children' or 'infants' (NASB, NRSV, NIV, ESV, AV) when 'child' would have sufficed. The treatment of women and children in the book of Nahum has rightly troubled many commentators, perhaps influencing their translations. In my reading of Nahum, all readers (including the original implied readers, whoever was intended) are supposed to be appalled by the fate of the children and good people in the fall of No-amon, as they are to be dismayed at the exposing of the prostitute, even though the latter is a metaphor in a way that the former were probably not.

It is unlikely that 'honourable' and 'great' men being treated badly (Nah. 3.10) is supposed to be read as anything other than troubling in a male-dominated society and in a text written by (almost certainly) a male, if not the words of a prophet named Nahum. The use of the male words for 'honourable' and 'great' do not exclude women, but here it is likely that men were meant, at least primarily. Furthermore, it is unlikely that any culture anywhere in the world at any time in history would not find the idea of children dashed to pieces (3.10) upsetting imagery. It is not unthinkable that, in the ANE as in the contemporary world, the image of hurting children would be more likely to elicit sympathy than would casting lots for honourable men. At any rate, together, the imagery of honourable men and children surely is intended to cause the audience of the text to feel sympathy and discomfort. The question is, To what purpose? The text of Nahum does not shy away from depicting the atrocities of war – good people and children are affected – and is a reminder of what the leaders (usually male, we know from our general knowledge) bring upon the innocent in their own country as well as others when they behave corruptly. How much of vv. 8-10 is intended to be metaphorical and how much is a straightforward account of what No-amon suffered is unclear. Either way, the book of Nahum strips war naked and shows it as it is for many who are caught up in it. That is, a key purpose of the book of Nahum is to portray an alarming picture. God rarely intervenes directly in the OT, but, instead, he works in and around the politics of countries and their wars. One country is used to punish another country, or God uses one country's military exploits against another, but that does not mean that he endorses the actions of the conquering party. The oracle against Babylon in Jeremiah 50 demonstrates this, for while God used Babylon against the other nations, he punishes her for what she has done to them (50.7, 15, 17–18, 29, 33–34; 51.24-25).

Garcia-Treto (1996: 603) writes of the image of a jealous and avenging God, 'Nahum's divine warrior is so deeply rooted in Judean nationalism, so intently focused on the utter destruction of the people's enemy that it is hard to imagine that, even for Nahum's time, that was all that could be said about God'. Quite clearly, 'even in Nahum's time', a lot more was said about God by other prophets that contrast the book of Nahum when taken at face value, but the book of Nahum itself says more with its focus on 'the utter destruction of the people's enemy'. Garcia-Treto's later claim of Nahum 'as the nationalistic poem that it clearly was for its author' (606) is problematic because it implies a blindness in the ancient (almost certainly) Jewish author(s) of Nahum to what they were writing.

Having outlined what happened to No-amon, Nah. 3.11-13 declares that the same sort of thing will happen to Nineveh. She will run in vain from her enemy, and her people and city will be weak against its onslaught. Some have seen the 'gates of your land are opened wide to your enemies' (Nah. 3.13) as a euphemism for a woman's vagina (e.g. Magdalene 2004: 333), but this reading seems a little forced in the context of the city's lack of security where 'gates' more naturally implies city gates. According to Cathcart (1973: 179–87), who builds on Hillers, some of the insults in Nahum, including vv. 11-15 are those of ANE treaty curses. The imagery of drunkenness being used in judgement is a common one in the prophets (e.g. Isa. 19.14, 49.26, 63.6; Jer. 13.13, 25.27, 48.26; and Ezek. 23.33). In fact, the language that is used for Nineveh is used elsewhere in the prophets for Judah and Israel. While this is to be expected given that oracles of judgement frequently depict war scenes, the familiar phrases and terms now used against Judah's enemies 'blur[s] the boundaries between "us" and "them"' (O'Brien 2002: 144). This is never so clear as in the question, 'Who will mourn for you?' in both Nah. 3.7 and Isa. 51.19, with both texts questioning that the falling city – Nineveh in Nahum and Jerusalem in Isaiah – could be comforted.

Locusts and stars

Verses 14-15 summon Nineveh to defend herself, but tell her that it will be futile. The end of v. 15 through to v. 17 uses the interesting double metaphor of the locust. Swarms of locusts were a perpetual threat and people were helpless before them; there was nothing anyone could do to prevent the damage that the locusts would do. The enemy's sword will be like a locust to Nineveh, but then she is called to try to become like a locust in return. In fact, it appears from v. 16 that she already has done so, for she has more traders than there are stars. Clearly, this is exaggerated language which should alert us to other exaggerated language in the book. Cat Quine observes (2019: 500) that this is the only time when God is not the one making people as numerous as the stars of the heavens and the only time when the people are not Israel. Furthermore, God made his people as numerous *as* the stars in the heaven, whereas the Ninevites had made themselves *more than* the stars of the heaven, an implicit act of hubris on the part of the Ninevites (Quine 2019: 500). The numerous people would look promising, except all her various locusts fly away and cannot be found by the time the sun has risen (3.17), so despite appearances, Nineveh's military situation is hopeless. Again, Quine (2019: 503) notes that it is ironic that the stars (which were normally depicted in Neo-Assyrian royal iconography as surrounding Ishtar) and the sun (the winged sun depicted Aššur) 'combine to symbolize its [Nineveh's] downfall'. The disappearance of the locusts is also ironic given that the Neo-Assyrian inscriptions depict the conquering Assyrian king and his army as a locust swarm. Like Gordon Johnston in his paper on the lion motif in Nahum (2001), Quine see the book of Nahum as deliberately using and inverting motifs and symbols used by the Neo-Assyrians for their self-identity, particularly in relation to kingship and power.

In addition to Nineveh's weakened military state, v. 18 castigates Nineveh's leaders for not doing their jobs; her people are scattered and the nation is actually in chaos. Or to use the word in v. 19, the nation is broken. In fact, she is broken beyond repair. Nineveh, as a city, is over, at least for now. Her irreversible breakdown and incurable wound is cause for rejoicing for those who have experienced and endured her cruelty. Except, as has been discussed, some of the language of Nahum is such that perhaps people will hesitate to clap their hands over her.

Nahum's theological purpose

Nahum's audiences

The OANs are addressed to – at least in places – the foreign nation. In that sense, the foreign nation would appear to be the implied audience. Given that they are in Israel's Scriptures, however, it is more likely that the implied audience is Israel/Judah, leaving the Ninevites as the putatively implied audience. Modern readers, particularly those for whom Nahum is Scripture, may read the spirit of the text with either of these implied audiences, even though the details do not match.

If one thinks of Nineveh as the implied audience, then Nahum's message might be that of most prophetic utterances. The prophet delivers his words and paints a bleak or horrible picture of the future in the hopes that the projection he gives is sufficiently awful that his audience (Nineveh) rethinks its lifestyle and repents, which would lead to God changing his mind about punishing the people – in the way that is outlined in Jeremiah 18. Jonah knew the purpose of prophecy, which is why he did not want to go to Nineveh – and in the book of Jonah, the Ninevites repented and were spared God's judgement. If the Ninevites in Nahum do not repent, however, then the punishment will weaken and disable them, preventing further cruelty. If one takes Israel and Judah as Nahum's intended implied audience, then the purpose of the book changes.

Dulce et decorum est

War has been glorified in countless ways and many a young soldier has confidently gone to war, excited and ready for action; usually action that – in the minds of the soldiers – is to set a wrong to rights and establish order. Nahum 1 through to 2.3 belongs to such young soldiers – and to those who watch from the sidelines, baying for the blood of the enemy. Nahum 1 is rousing and one can imagine that it elicits loud 'Amens' from those who want justice and retribution for the wrongs done to them and for the oppressing nation to be obliterated. The first hint of a change of tone is in 2.4 where the realities of war appear to be quite different to the expected outcome given the picture of the day of preparation in the previous verse, for 2.3 is a stirring vision where everything seems bright and shiny, and newly uniformed soldiers, well-armed and provisioned are ready for combat. The depiction of combat that immediately follows, however, shows a very different picture: chariots racing madly in the streets and rushing wildly. The reality of a battle is chaos.

The poet and soldier Wilfred Owen is credited as being one of the first poets, following Sassoon, to portray war in its true colours (Stallworthy 1984: xxviii). His brutal imagery of reality shocks. In his famous poem, '*Dulce et Decorum Est*', he bitterly exclaims that people would not encourage 'children ardent for some desperate glory' to go to war with the lie that it is sweet and decorous/glorious/honourable to die for one's country ('*Dulce et decorum est pro patria mori*') (Stallworthy 1984: 189), if they had witnessed for themselves the horrific, nightmarish experience. Nahum's poetry is not too dissimilar. Desiring the obliteration of an enemy involves the reality of war and the suffering of the 'innocent' – handmaidens (2.7), children (3.10) and honourable and great men (3.10). What looks to be a positive account of God's vengeance in Nahum 1 fast becomes more like an anti-war treatise in the manner of Owen's poetry. One cannot have vengeance without brutal bloodshed.

García-Treto (1996: 611) considers that 'Nahum in all probability did not intend to arouse in his readers empathy and pity for the people of Nineveh, but he comes close, with his skill in description, to making it inevitable and to strengthening the case against violence'. What makes García-Treto conclude that Nahum 'in all probability' did not intend to arouse sympathy? My conclusion is the opposite. What writer in any time and place in history does not think that an account of children being dashed to pieces will not invoke an immediate gut reaction of recoiling horror, sympathy and outrage? Elisha wept because he foresaw the pain and destruction that Hazael would bring to Israel, including children being dashed to pieces and pregnant women ripped open (2 Kgs 8.11-12). Such depictions in Nahum are surely a deliberate ploy to stop in their tracks those who are seeking vengeance and who want every last Ninevite individual dead, whatever it takes. Nahum makes it clear that such things have happened before. It is, as García-Treto comes close to saying, more akin to an anti-war treatise. Are those who called for justice and vengeance in Nahum 1 still saying, 'Amen' by the end of the book? This purpose of Nahum's vision, therefore, is to make those seeking vengeance question how much they really want God's vengeance to fall on this enemy.

Goldingay (2006: 609) makes the point that the psalmist who authored Ps. 137.9 'appeals to the words of prophets' (as well as Nah. 3.10, see Hos. 10.14, 13.16) which are 'a recurrent OT image for what happens in war' (609). He also explores the idea (2006: 611–12), citing Athalya Brenner, Primo Levi and P. D. James, that there are extreme occasions when people might want a God of vengeance. The psalmist of 137.9 who desires that Babylon's little ones be dashed against a rock (if this is not to be taken metaphorically) sees in that a repayment for what Babylon has done to them (v. 8). All these passages play into the same thinking and discussion about vengeance – an honest declaration of desire that children killed cruelly be properly avenged, the brutal reality of what that entails and the weeping over it. Arguably, Elisha's tears are in a different context, because Elisha has not been wronged by Hazael and Hazael will not be acting in vengeance, though Hazael is one who starts a chain of pain that requires vengeance. War and vengeance are ugly and the OT portrays them as such, but it also allows for strong sentiments to be expressed in the context of prayer (Ps. 137.9) and Nahum's prophecy.

A voice for the oppressed

Indeed, while Nahum's strong language is abhorrent to most readers and hearers, it may have provided comfort to the house of Jacob who had suffered under Assyria, by giving them an outlet. That is, there may have been some for whom Nahum's words were welcome and provided emotional relief. As vivid and brutal as that outlet is, it keeps it to the written or spoken word.

> Is it possible that a mighty power like the Assyrians will ever fall? Yet in language that actually taunts the enemy, it is prophesied that this cruel rule of the Assyrian Empire will come to an end. In this way, hope is given to people in a seemingly hopeless situation. By giving them this hope, Nahum, true to his name, brings comfort to his people. Thus, Assyria and its capital refer here to more than simply a world power sometime during the seventh century BC; they become a symbol of all oppressive political powers that take away other people's freedom and dignity. (Snyman 2020: 44)

Nahum finishes with, 'For on whom has not your evil passed continually?' and this ending is recognition of the devastation that Nineveh had caused so many people. Nahum has taken seriously Nineveh's crimes against humanity. Reading Nahum as an anti-war poem does not deny a voice to those who called on God's vengeance.

Concluding remarks: Nahum for everybody

García-Treto (1996: 596) points out that 'Nahum shares with Obadiah the dubious distinction of being the only prophetic books that do not appear in the Revised Common Lectionary, and probably for similar reasons'. All Souls Church, Langham Place, London, a well-known, large, Anglican Church, which is part of the Evangelical Alliance, has digitized all its recorded sermons going back to 1971 or possibly earlier. They would assert that 'all Scripture is God-breathed...' (1 Tim. 3.16-17) and yet in over half a century of recordings, a quick search for 'Nahum' brings up only one recorded sermon on Nahum (preached by Richard Bewes in 1988). Nahum is the only book of the Christian Bible to have been preached just once. Anecdotal information from Jewish colleagues tells the same story – Nahum is no more popular in the synagogue than he is in the churches - 'no lectionary reading has been taken from the Book of Nahum, as if implying that it does not have anything ethical or theological to offer of the same caliber as the other prophets' (Pinker 2004: 148). Since these disturbing verses in Nahum, along with other difficult biblical texts, are part of the canon for Jews and Christians, it is arguably more responsible for scholars to try to work with the texts than to dismiss them, not least in order to strive to serve these religious adherents who are clearly struggling with these texts.

Some, like Ralph Smith (1984: 68) consider that Nahum's 'real message' is 'to stress the sovereignty of God over history and the world. God is good and just.' The fact that many (most?) believers of two of the world's major religions resist these verses, however, demonstrates that their religions have shaped them enough that they recognize the problematic nature of Nahum. The book of Nahum presents difficult issues so starkly that it is difficult for them to be ignored. Jews and Christians down through the ages have not liked the book of Nahum for a good reason; it is not supposed to be liked.

I have argued that Nahum is an extended anti-war poem and in hearing or reading it, a victim is faced with the question of how much they want their perpetrator to suffer. It seems plausible that at least some among the original implied audiences in hearing, 'Who will grieve for her?' might have thought that perhaps they would grieve at least for the innocent who would be caught up in Nineveh's downfall. It is an implicit reversal of Abraham pleading for Sodom and Gomorrah, asking God if he would still punish the cities even if there were a few righteous people in them – and trying to ascertain how few righteous people there need to be before God withheld his punishment. Nahum's implicit question, in contrast, is to ask the victim how much they want the oppressive nation to suffer. It is not emotional blackmail, not least because it is only implicit, but encourages a serious thinking through of what a nation's punishment looks like, that is, that innocent people will suffer. Nor does there need to be a right or wrong answer. Some, who have lost many and been deeply damaged by Nineveh might applaud Nahum's words and find them cathartic. The process in thinking where God's vengeance should stop is valuable in and of itself. Those of us who have not been terrorized by war and our families decimated probably understand Nahum the least – which maybe one reason it is not chosen as a text to be preached in the UK at least.

Gitay (1995: 206) writes of Jonah, 'The issue is how to relate to hated enemies who wounded Israel almost mortally given that a number of prophets and psalmists (see also Ps. 137) called for divine revenge.' It is usual to link Jonah and Nahum because both relate to Nineveh and many (with relief) read Nahum in the light of Jonah. It is useful to read both books together as a thought-experiment. In Jonah, there is no punishment for Nineveh. In Nahum, there is nothing but punishment. Where does the reader sit in terms of what God's grace and vengeance should look like? Is the book of Jonah too lenient with Nineveh and the book of Nahum too harsh? This will be more than a thought-experiment for those who, with Judah, resonate with 'for on whom has not your evil passed continuously' (Nah. 3.19) – those who have suffered atrocities under oppressive regimes. For them, the question possibly has existential urgency. Such readers who genuinely battle with the idea of vengeance because of horrific wrongs done to them, their family or their country may find it helpful to start with Jonah and Nahum as a basis upon which to build, in working out their own approach. Jonah and Nahum are the only two books of the OT to end with a rhetorical question. In both cases, God is the questioner, but each is quite different in nature. In Jonah, God asks if he should not have compassion on Nineveh and in Nahum he asks, 'For on whom has not your evil passed continually?' The two questions together probe deeply the existential issue of compassion versus vengeance/punishment. Kim (2007: 510) also concludes that, 'Each is meant to challenge the theological outlook of the other. Perhaps that is why both Jonah and Nahum conclude with a question'. Both Jonah and, to a greater extent, probably, Nahum engage the emotions and to read those books while taking one's pulse might be fruitful in determining the starting point for the reader. Jonah and Nahum together might have their place in reconciliation programmes (many of which are Christian) that are going on in various countries of the world.

The response to Nahum's war-vision might be varied, in the way that people's feelings about war are complex. Nancy Sherman has done much work with soldiers who have seen action and she writes in the prologue to *The Untold War* (2011: 3), 'Soldiers are genuinely torn by the feelings of war – they desire raw revenge at times, though they wish they wanted a nobler justice; they feel pride and patriotism tinged with shame, complicity, betrayal, and guilt'.

Ultimately, the book of Nahum is a vision – a picture – and people will undoubtedly respond to it differently, depending on their circumstances. While most people advise taking Jonah and Nahum together and Nahum follows Jonah in the LXX, they are not together in the MT canon. Micah comes between them. Micah, in my understanding, plays its own role in the question of justice.

References

Achtemeier, Elizabeth (1986). *Nahum – Malachi, Interpretation*. Atlanta, GA: John Knox.

Baker, David W. (1988). *Nahum, Habakkuk and Zephaniah*, Tyndale Old Testament Commentaries, 17–40. Leicester: IVP.

Bewes, Richard, 'The Prophet of Retribution – Nahum', Series: *Majoring on the Minors*. Recorded: 07 August 1988. https://www.allsouls.org/Media/AllMedia.aspx (accessed 07 January 2025).

Calvin, J. (2005). *Commentaries on the Twelve Minor Prophets*, vol. 2, trans. J. Owen. Grand Rapids MI: Baker Books.

Cathcart, Kevin J. (1973). 'Treaty-Curses and the Book of Nahum'. *Catholic Biblical Quarterly*, 35 (2): 179–87.

Christensen, Duane L. (2009). *Nahum: A New Translation with Introduction and Commentary*, The Anchor Yale Bible 24F. New Havens: Yale University Press.

Clark, David J., and Howard A. Hatton (1989). *A Translator's Handbook on the Books of Nahum, Habakkuk, and Zephaniah*, Helps for Translators. New York: United Bible Societies.

Coggins, Richard J. (1985). 'Nahum', in Richard J. Coggins and S. Paul Re'emi (eds), *Nahum, Obadiah, Esther: Israel among the Nations*, International Theological Commentary, 1–63. Grand Rapids, MI: Eerdmans / Edinburgh: Handsel Press.

Cook, Gregory D. (2016). 'Nahum and the Question of Rape'. *Bulletin for Biblical Research*, 26 (3): 341–52.

Dempsey Carol (2021). 'Metaphor in the Minor Prophets', in Julia M. O'Brien (ed.), *Oxford Handbook to Minor Prophets*, 85–100. New York: Oxford University Press.

García-Treto, Francisco O. (1996). 'Nahum', in Leander E. Keck, Thomas G. Long, Bruce C. Birch, Katheryn Pfisterer Darr, William L. Lane, Gail

R. O'Day, David L. Petersen, John J. Collins, Jack A. Keller Jr, James Earl Massey, Marrion L. Soards (eds), *Introduction to Apocalyptic Literature, Daniel, The Twelve Prophets*, Vol. 7 of *The New Interpreter's Bible: A Commentary in Twelve Volumes*, 591–619. Nashville, TN: Abingdon Press.

Gitay, Yehoshua (1995). 'Jonah: The Prophecy of Antirhetoric', in Astrid B. Beck, Andrew H. Bartelt, Paul R. Raabe, Chris A. Franke (eds), *Fortunate the Eyes That See: Essays in Honor of David Noel Freedman in Celebration of His Seventieth Birthday*, 197–206. Grand Rapids, MI / Cambridge: William B. Eerdmans.

Goldingay, J. (2006). *Psalms 90–150, vol. 3*, Baker Commentary on the Old Testament. Grand Rapids, MI: Baker Academic.

Gordon, Pamela, and Harold C. Washington (1995). 'Rape as a Military Metaphor in the Hebrew Bible', in Athalya Brenner (ed.), *A Feminist Companion to the Minor Prophets, Vol. 8, A Feminist Companion to the Bible*, 308–25. London: T&T Clark.

Grayson, A. K. (2008). 'Assyria 668–635 B.C.: The Reign of Ashurbanipal', in John Boardman (ed.), *The Cambridge Ancient History*, Vol. 3, Part II, 142–61. Cambridge Histories Online, Cambridge University Press.

'A Hymn to Inana as Ninegala (Inana D)', in Electronic Text Corpus of Sumerian Literature. https://etcsl.orinst.ox.ac.uk/cgi-bin/etcsl.cgi?text=t.4.07.4# (accessed 13 August 2024).

Jerome (2016). *Commentaries on the Twelve Prophets*, vol. 1, T. P. Scheck, T. C. Oden, & G. L. Bray (eds), Ancient Christian Texts. Downers Grove, IL: IVP Academic.

Johnston, Gordon II. (2001). 'Nahum's Rhetorical Allusions to the Neo-Assyrian Lion Motif'. *Bibliotheca Sacra* 158: 287–307.

Kim, Hyun Chul Paul (2007). 'Jonah Read Intertextually'. *Journal of Biblical Literature*, 126 (3): 497–528.

Longman III, Tremper (1993). 'Nahum', in Thomas Edward McComiskey (ed.), *The Minor Prophets: An Exegetical and Expository Commentary*, Vol. 2. Grand Rapids, MI: Baker Academic.

Magdalene, F. Rachel (2004). 'Ancient Near Eastern Treaty-Curses and the Ultimate Texts of Terror: A Study of the Language of Divine Sexual Abuse in the Prophetic Corpus', in Athalya Brenner (ed.), *A Feminist Companion to the Minor Prophets, Vol. 8, A Feminist Companion to the Bible*, 326–52. London: T&T Clark.

Maier, Walter A. (1980). *The Book of Nahum: A Commentary*, Thornapple Commentaries. Grand Rapids, MI: Baker Academic.

Mark, Joshua J. (2014). *Ashurnasirpal II*, section 'Early Reign and Military Campaigns', *Ancient History Encyclopaedia*. https://www.ancient.eu/Ashurnasirpal_II/ (accessed 28 May 2024).

O'Brien, Julia Myers (2002). *Nahum*. New York: Sheffield Academic Press.
Ogden, Graham S. (2023). *Nahum, Habakkuk, and Malachi*. Readings: A New Biblical Commentary, Sheffield: Sheffield Phoenix Press.
Pinker, Aron (2004). 'Nahum's Theological Perspectives', *JBQ*, 32: 148–57.
Quine, Cat (2019). 'Nineveh's Pretensions to Divine Power in Nahum 3:16'. *Vetus Testamentum*, 69 (3): 498–504.
Renz, T. (2021). *The Books of Nahum, Habakkuk, and Zephaniah*, NICOT. Grand Rapids, MI: William B. Eerdmans.
Sherman, Nancy (2011). *The Untold War: Inside the Hearts, Minds, and Souls of Our Soldiers*, Reprint edn. New York: W. W. Norton.
'A šir-namšub to Inana (Inana I)', in Electronic Text Corpus of Sumerian Literature. https://etcsl.orinst.ox.ac.uk/cgi-bin/etcsl.cgi?text=t.4.07.9# (accessed 13 August 2024).
Smith, John Merlin Powis, J. A. ([1911] 1965). 'Nahum', in John Merlin Powis Smith, William Hayes Ward and Julius A. Bewer (eds), *A Critical and Exegetical Commentary, on Micah, Zephaniah, Nahum, Habakkuk, Obadiah and Joel*, International Critical Commentary on the Holy Scriptures of the Old and New Testaments, 265–360. Edinburgh: T&T Clark.
Smith, Ralph L. (1984). *Micah – Malachi*, Word Biblical Commentary 32. Waco, TX: Word Books.
Snyman, S. D. (2020). *Nahum, Habakkuk and Zephaniah: An Introduction and Commentary*, Vol. 27. Downers Grove, IL: IVP Academic.
Stallworthy, Jon, ed. (1984). *The Oxford Book of War Poetry*. Oxford: Oxford University Press.
Sweeney, M. A. (2000). *The Twelve Prophets*, Vols 1 & 2 of *Berit Olam: Studies in Hebrew Narrative and Poetry*, D. W. Cotter, J. T. Walsh, and C. Franke (eds). Collegeville, MN: Liturgical Press.
Watts, John D. W. (1975). *The Books of Joel, Obadiah, Jonah, Nahum, Habakkuk, and Zephaniah*, The Cambridge Bible Commentary on the New English Bible. London: Cambridge University Press.

4

Micah

Introduction

Jonah and Nahum are both books that are short enough to be dealt with in relative detail, chapter by chapter. Micah with its seven chapters is a little long for such a treatment in a work of this length and so this chapter on Micah will be structured differently. Various aspects of the book of Micah will be dealt with under the headings that follow with the final section reserved for a brief overview of contemporary writers on Micah, particularly those who bring existential questions to the text. In the main, I have chosen to do this with a paragraph or two on selected texts throughout Micah. To begin, however, we look at the historical-critical background of Micah and then its literary significance, particularly the canonical position that Micah has between Jonah and Nahum.

Historical and geographical setting

Historical setting

The book of Micah begins by giving the historical setting of the prophet Micah's words as 'in the days of Jotham, Ahaz and Hezekiah, kings of Judah' (Mic. 1.1). Jotham reigned from 742 to 735 BCE, Ahaz from 735 to 715 BCE, and Hezekiah from 715 to 686 BCE. This likely places Micah historically between Jonah and Nahum. As many scholars have noted (e.g. Coomber 2021: 208; Simundson 1996: 534; Waltke 1993: 591–2), the neo-Assyrian Empire rose to its height during this mid- to late-century period and expanded into the southern Levant, Judah becoming a vassal state of Assyria in the reign of Ahaz. The Levant roughly refers to the countries along the eastern coast of the Mediterranean Sea but includes adjacent neighbouring countries further inland. Vassalage brought huge changes to Judah, Coomber (2021: 208–9) explains, including massive population growth; immensely increased fortification to Jerusalem and other areas; and introduction of standardized weights and measures, along with important agricultural reforms such as irrigation systems and dams which enabled previously infertile areas to be farmed. The area became rich in olive oil, wine and fruit. As well, luxury goods were being imported. Such development and expansion required policies, administration and management which led to a new, wealthy, landowning class which abused its position and oppressed the poorer masses (Dempsey 2015: 105–6). These social injustices form a key component of Micah's teaching. Dempsey (2015: 105) considers that the prophet's career was probably limited to the last quarter of the century during Hezekiah's reign between the Syro-Ephraimite War in 734–732 BCE and Sennacherib's invasion of Judah in 701 BCE.

Who is Micah?

Classic midrash is more concerned with imaginative intertextual moves than with context of origin and Simkovich (2021: 235) interestingly and helpfully summarizes some of these rabbinic traditions. Conventionally, Micah was seen as the Micah who hires a young Levite to serve as his idolatrous priest in Judg. 17–18. Rabbinic legends thus portray Micah as an idolater who left Egypt with the Israelites, perhaps even making his idol from Egyptian silver. Other traditions portray Micah more positively and recount that when the angels wanted to destroy his idol, God stopped them because Micah had been hospitable to travellers.

Another possibility – which considers that his name comes from the word meaning 'crush' – sees Micah as one of the babies who, according to tradition, was crushed into a building when the Israelites were forced to use their own children as brickwork (Simkovich 2021: 235). In this scenario, Micah was saved by Moses. In still other traditions, Micah is equated with Sheba the son of Bichri or with Nebat the father of Jeroboam (Simkovich 2021: 235).

Geographical setting

Micah 1.1 says that Micah was from Moresheth and 1.14 refers to Moresheth-Gath. It is not clear how Moresheth-Gath should be translated or what the relationship between the two words is, but it is usually interpreted nowadays as Moresheth of Gath, Moresheth being the smaller area within Gath. Moresheth or Moresheth-Gath was in the Shephelah which Phillips (2022: 173–4) explains was a lowland area that was part of the western foothills of the mountains that ran from the coast to the interior. Mays points out that the prophets Micah and Nahum are both introduced as being from a particular place, rather than as a son of their fathers – Micah the Moreshite and Nahum the Elkoshite (Mays 1976: 15). These are the only two prophets introduced in this way: most are introduced with their fathers' names, a few with their name only, and Amos is described as being among the sheepherders from Tekoa.

Micah was from Moresheth in the time that Judah was under Assyrian vassalage, but he directed his prophecies to both the northern kingdom of Israel and the southern kingdom of Judah, particularly the key city of each – Samaria and Jerusalem, respectively. Micah prophesied that Samaria would be made a heap of ruins and her foundations uncovered (1.6) which Kessler (2021: 466) understands as the final end of Samaria – and, in fact, Samaria is not mentioned again in the canonical sequence of the Twelve in the MT, so in a literary sense in the MT, Mic. 1.6 is the end of Samaria. Since Samaria was rebuilt soon after it was destroyed, however, Kessler makes the point that Samaria's destruction is a theological concept. That is, as far as God was concerned, the northern kingdom of Israel had come to an end. In contrast, Kessler continues, Jerusalem's destruction is not definitive and in fact from 4.1, Zion is the highest of the mountains and Jerusalem the centre of the world. Again, this is a theological concept and a reminder that while geographical place names are useful in setting the scene for contemporary readers, they are not always the key places in the prophecy itself, which is theological by nature. Zimran (2021: 6) notes that 'Zion', referring to the place or the people, occurs nine times in Mic. 1-4 but does not appear in the rest of the book. 'Jerusalem' appears eight times in its geographical and national sense in the book of Micah but only in chs 1, 3 and 4. Three times Jerusalem parallels Zion and twice it is in parallel with Samaria.

Dating

Although the content of Micah points to a setting in the mid-to-late eighth century because its superscription in 1.1 dates the prophesies of Micah to the kings of Jotham, Ahaz and Hezekiah, the book was likely to have been transmitted orally and then written later. The superscription is commonly thought to be a later addition (e.g. Kessler 2021: 463; John Merlin Powis Smith 1911: 31; Ralph Smith 1984: 13; Simundson 1996: 542) which means that Micah could have been written earlier, though the general consensus of scholarship settles on a date for the composition/compilation in the exilic or postexilic periods (Coomber 2021: 208; Kessler 2021: 464–5). As with most of the biblical books, however, the composition of the final form of Micah would have had its own complex journey and scholars propose different dates for various layers in the text. Some of the questions that have been asked and debated are the following: whether the superscription in 1.1 is supposed to apply to the whole book; which the oldest parts of the book are; and whether these oldest texts date back to Micah and his followers – along with the corollary question about which authors and editors wrote which parts. Coomber (2021: 208) posits that any eighth-century materials were heavily redacted. Since Bernhard Stade in 1881, scholars have often seen Mic. 1–3 as the nucleus of the book's composition (Kessler 2021: 463) with chs 4–7 being written by later authors. The nations that stream to Zion in peace in Mic. 4.1-4 suggest to scholars such as Phillips (2022: 184) a postexilic context for Mic. 4–7.

Micah has the unique honour of being a prophet who is quoted as authoritative by another prophet, for Mic. 3.12 is quoted in Jer. 26.18. Not only does this make it clear that Micah precedes Jeremiah here (notwithstanding later editors of Jeremiah), but Jer. 26.18 helpfully provides a date for this verse that is absent in Micah's source material, for there is no mention of 'in the days of Hezekiah' in Mic. 3.12. Jeremiah 26.17-19 suggests, Phillips (2022: 184) says, that all or most of what precedes Mic. 3.12 would have been known in Hezekiah's time 'at the latest'. Nevertheless, scholars do not know when the eighth-century prophetic oracles were assembled and it could have been as early as the end of Hezekiah's reign or as late as the second-century BCE (Phillips 2022: 184).

Most academic commentaries, including those quoted above, give overviews of issues of dating for those who wish to explore the subject further. Halvorson-Taylor's chapter in *In the Shadow of Empire* (2021) would be a good place to start in terms of thinking about the wider issues concerned with dating. She summarizes scholarly efforts to date Micah's layers based on texts of destruction and consolation against the fall of Judah to Babylon in 586/587 and also elucidates the problems with attempts to date those layers (2021: 97–101). Studying the literary artistry, namely the 'seams' between the earlier texts of destruction and the later restoration passages in Mic. 4.8–5.2, she concludes that rather than being 'seams' that link the preceding and following passages, they indicate start and end points (first passage Mic. 4.9-10 and second passage Mic. 4.11-13). That is, the text 'appears, in other words, to overrule itself synchronically in the manner that some have read the relationship between oracles of destruction and consolation diachronically' (2021: 101). She goes on to argue that in using familiar language for different purposes and by use of redirection, the text is powerful 'for both acknowledging the current crisis and, simultaneously, indicating that it is not all that it seems – or, at least, not forever' (113). In addition, Micah's oracles were intentionally redacted in a way that they could be used for future audiences in different contexts, for 'the historical ties are loose' (113); for example, it is not always possible to determine whether it is Assyria, Babylon or another empire that is in view.

Coming from a different perspective, Jason Radine addresses the identical passages of Mic. 4.1-4 and Isa. 2.2-4 in terms of dating. If one draws on the other, then establishing one date can help establish the other (and the same would be true of other highly similar passages).

> Caution is advisable however in perceiving identical or very close wording as a case of intertextuality and dependence. Even at its most literate, both pre- and postexilic Israel/Judah/Yehud was a mostly oral society, from which the written Hebrew Bible is only the tip of the iceberg. Expressions such as these duplicate passages could have been fairly common sayings or axioms in society. (Radine 2021: 21–2).

Stansell (1988: 5) makes it clear that 'since Micah and Isaiah were contemporaries, the question of *literary* dependence of one upon the other does not bear any significance'.

Translations

Before turning to the literary aspect of Micah, it is worth a quick glance at the ancient translations of Micah. Phillips (2022: 188) notes that while the MT text of Micah is quite well preserved, the meaning is not always clear and thus early translations (LXX, Tg, Syr and Vg) vary significantly. 'When the LXX translators misunderstood the text, they attempted to make paraphrastic sense of it.'

Micah is rarely cited in Second Temple Jewish literature, but small fragments of a *pesher* on Micah were found at Qumran. A quick explanation of a *pesher* is that it is an interpretative comment. Our earliest, clearest examples are from and relate to the Qumran community. The Qumran *pesher* fragments on Micah reappropriate Micah's condemnations of Samaria in Mic. 1.5-6 to be condemnations of the 'Spouter of Lies' in their own day and they see Mic. 1.5's reference to Jerusalem as the 'high place' of Judah as speaking of the Teacher of Righteousness (Simkovich 2021: 234–5).

Literary artistry and structure

Literary artistry

A number of scholars have seen a literary artistry to the final form of Micah and have perceived and written upon a wide range of literary aspects. For example, Andersen and Freedman (2000: 564), basing their work on Andersen's 1994 chapter 'The Poetic Properties of Prophetic Discourse in the Book of Micah' in *Biblical Hebrew and Discourse Linguistics* (ed. Robert D. Bergen) note that 'shorter colons go with the agitation of more emotional discourse'. Another example is Elaine Phillips (2022: 183) who notes that all discourse units are within an inclusio and she (with many others) points out that the book of Micah begins in 1.1 with Micah's name, a shortened form of the name Micayahu normally rendered Micaiah in the English (e.g. Jer. 36.11, 13) meaning 'Who is like YHWH?', and ends with the question, 'Who is a God like you?' in 7.18.

Carol Dempsey (2021: 89) sums up the works of Anne Moore (2009), Walter Brueggemann (1981), Pierre J. P. Van Hecke (2003), and Juan Cruz (2016) who all look at metaphor in the book of Micah. Moore focuses on the metaphor of 'king' in Micah and Zephaniah, Brueggemann sees Mic. 4.1-5 as using metaphor to evoke an alternative worldview, van Hecke looks at the pastoral metaphors in Mic. 7.14 and Cruz examines the divine metaphors across the whole book. Dempsey comments, however, that 'none of them deal with the metaphors' cognitive and conceptual aspects nor the effects the metaphors have on readers and the contemporary world' (89) and she exhorts scholars to read against the grain of the text to challenge prejudices (96–7).

Stansell (1988) compares and contrasts various traditions in Micah and Isaiah (contemporaries of each other). He argues that both prophets would have been familiar with the theophanic tradition ('theophanies' being appearances of God on earth/to humans, such as in the burning bush), likewise the Jerusalem and Zion tradition, prophetic conflict and opposition, and social critique. While both prophets were acquainted with ancient Israelite traditions, each adapts the tradition and reworks it for his own purposes (133). For instance, Micah radically reverses the motif of the theophanic tradition so that instead of the LORD coming to save, he comes to judge (133). While both view Jerusalem's leadership as corrupt and Jerusalem as under the LORD's wrath, in Micah, the city will not simply fall but be annihilated because of its leaders (133). At the same time, 'not once does Micah place Judah alongside Jerusalem in his accusations of guilt' (134). Micah's and Isaiah's social critique are also similar, but Micah only uses words of accusation and judgement and there is no room in his sayings for an admonition to do justice (134–5), 'nor is there any hint or suggestion that Micah calls for repentance' (135). In these ways, therefore, it becomes clear that the prophets and their authors intentionally shaped their material, so that each book has a unique literary artistry of its own. Some have posited the idea that it was written as a dramatic performance (see Dempster 2017: 47–8). I expand a little more on the issues Stansell raises in the section 'Micah in the Contemporary World' with respect to Yisca Zimran's paper on Isaiah and Micah, and Jamie Banister's monologue on theophanies. For now, though, I continue to look at literary artistry, though under slightly narrower headings.

Genre and form

In studying the genres and forms in the minor prophets, Floyd (2021: 77) groups Hosea, Joel, Amos, Obadiah, Micah and Zephaniah into a category which he describes as typological books. They have the same elements: oracles of punishment described in terms of defeat and exile; oracles renewing the LORD's relationship with his people, 'in the context of an often violent transformation of the world order' (77); and restoration of the LORD's people to a land where they can dwell in safety, security and prosperity. The above prophetic books may concentrate on one of these elements, be creative in their use or have them in different orders, but the third element of restoration always comes last, even if it has occurred earlier in the book.

Halvorson-Taylor (2021: 97–101) looks at how the exile is depicted in the poetry of Micah and makes the pertinent observation about genre when she says of information provided via poetry that it 'may be less "historical," but it is no less culturally significant' (99).

James Trotter (2015: 63–74) calls into question the assumption that the familiar trope of the prophetic lawsuit would have had any meaning to Persian Jehudite readers and argues that it is 'highly unlikely' (72) they would have associated it with the law courts. He uses texts from Hosea and Micah, but particularly states that he does not address the question about how Hosea's and Micah's original audiences would have heard them.

Structure and coherence

In his PhD dissertation, Cuffey spends a few pages outlining the main viewpoints that have been proposed for the structure of Micah: four-part structure (A. Weiser); threefold (B. Childs, R. Smith, J. Willis, W. Rudolph, L. C. Allen and H. W. Wolff); and two (J. L. Mays and D. G. Hagstrom) though he notes that scholars divide in different places even if they agree on the number of divisions – this is particularly the case for those who divide Micah into three sections (Cuffey 1987: 178–84). Cuffey himself divides Micah into four (1.2–2.13, 3.1–4.8, 4.9–5.15, 6.1–7.20) (245–88) but is more concerned with showing the coherence of Micah.

Kessler (2021: 461) speaks for many when he says that the change between doom and hope in Micah is what leads scholars to suggest a threefold division. Dempster (2017: 24–5) sees chs 1–2, 3–5 and 6–7 'like the three movements of a musical score, with the second and third movements gradually increasing in intensity and volume as the score progresses, with the dark night of judgement gradually fading as the dawn of grace approaches'. Andersen and Freedman (2008: 7) structure the book slightly differently: the book of doom (1.2–3.12), the book of visions (4.1–5.15) and the book of contention and conciliation (6.1–7.20). They see the books as 'marked by well-formed beginnings, with each ending on a note of finality (3:12; 5:14; 7:20)' (7). Kessler's own summary is that

> There are good arguments for every proposal concerning the structure of the book, be it twofold, threefold, or fourfold, each with variations in itself. One need not discuss them as strict alternatives. Indeed, "there is no definitive

way to outline the book" (Smith 1984, 8 n. 4). Like in a piece of music, it is possible to hear different voices at the same time. In chapters 1–3, a voice of lament is dominant, but it is interrupted in 2.12–13 by another voice that is hopeful. Micah 2:12–13 introduces a theme that is taken up again in 4:6–7. Between 3:12 and 4:1 one finds something like a general pause. Micah 6:9–15 with its accusations against the rich in some way sounds like a reprise of the denouncements in chapter 2. (2021: 462)

Cuffey is not the only one to search for coherence in Micah, and Kessler (2021: 462) pinpoints the 1980s as the starting point for this interest. David Hagstrom (1988) in his PhD thesis demonstrates persuasively that 'the book of Micah in its final form displays such coherence as to be capable of being construed as a unit' (125). It is undoubtedly the choppy nature of the text which has caused many to struggle with Micah in its final form and which has then been the driving force for these scholars to find coherence. Again, to summarize Kessler (2021: 463), 'Evaluating the competing approaches and results, one should admit that a book like that of Micah has structures that overlay each other, producing different coherences on the respective levels.'

Micah in the twelve

Matthew 2.5 introduces a citation from Mic. 5.2 with 'this is what has been written by the prophet'. Shepherd (2021: 245) comments that it is not clear if 'the prophet' is Micah or whether it refers to 'someone responsible for the Book of the Twelve'. He nevertheless concludes from his study of citations of the Twelve that 'for the New Testament authors and those most deeply influenced by them, the Book of the Twelve was more than a collection of separate books' (249).

Sweeney (2021: 273) states that Jewish interpreters have tended to read the Twelve as one book with twelve elements, whereas Christian interpreters have been inclined to see them as Twelve individual books. Sieges (2021: 29–38) gives a good account of how the book of the Twelve was seen as one entity by early Jewish and Christian interpreters, then came to be seen as twelve individual books and in the 1990s started to be viewed again as a single unit. Nogalski (diachronic approach) and House (synchronic approach) are the two names from the 1990s at the forefront of this renewed interest in the twelve books being linked, though other names from this decade include Terence Collins and Richard Coggins. Nogalski considered Hosea, Amos,

Micah and Zephaniah to have been edited together during the exile and these became known as 'The Book of the Four'. Sweeney (2021: 274) sees the interest in considering the Twelve as one book as starting with Budde's work in 1922 – Budde was interested in the dual nature of the books in the Twelve as individual entities as well as part of a whole. Budde was followed by Ronald E. Wolfe in 1935 and Dale Schneider in 1979.

The order of the books in the Twelve differs between the MT and the LXX. The order in MT is Hosea, Joel, Amos, Obadiah, Jonah, Micah, Nahum, Habakkuk, Zephaniah, Haggai, Zechariah and Malachi. The order of the first six in the LXX is Hosea, Amos, Micah, Joel, Obadiah and Jonah. The order of the last six books is the same in LXX and MT. It is often thought that the Twelve are ordered chronologically and it may be that differences of opinion regarding which ones came first caused the variation in order. Alternatively, as Glenny (2015: 2) notes, the arrangement may have been due to length – or other factors.

Glenny (2015: 2–3) observes that Hosea, Amos and Micah all deal with northern Israel and Samaria though each is also concerned with Judah and Jerusalem. Micah and Joel (the book that follows Micah in LXX) are connected by the Zion tradition. Although the nations are gathered to Jerusalem in both Micah and Joel, in Micah it is for peace whereas in Joel it is for judgement. Glenny's work is to be recommended as one of the few commentaries that deal with the LXX version of Micah.

Micah is one of the books that varies most in its positioning between MT and LXX and Glenny (2015: 3) writes:

> The fact that the arrangement of the Twelve in the LXX differs from the arrangement in the Hebrew Bible is important for the interpretation of LXX Mic, because Mic is one of the books that differs most in its position in the LXX from its position in the Hebrew Bible. In Mic the judgment on Samaria and northern Israel is a lesson and warning for Jerusalem and Judah, and in the LXX arrangement of Hos, Amos, and Mic the progression of the LORD's dealings with his people moves directly from the north to the south before attention is turned to the nations.

Micah's different positioning not only affects its interpretation in the LXX but in the MT as well. One of the key significances is that in LXX, Jonah is followed by Nahum whereas in MT, Micah comes between them. For the many scholars who advise reading Jonah and Nahum together, the LXX's order is convenient and there is no real need to deal with Micah in relation to Jonah and Nahum. For those (the majority) who are following the MT, however, and also wish to deal with Jonah and Nahum together, it is less easy: they need to take account of the fact that Micah sits between them.

Micah between Jonah and Nahum in MT

House sees the Twelve going through a sin-punishment-restoration cycle and Micah is the last of the section (Hosea to Micah) which demonstrates that Israel and Judah have sinned. He (House 1990: 139) remarks, however, that 'Scholars rarely agree on Micah's structure, so it is not surprising that Micah's own plot and its place in the Twelve are not easy to define'. In House's opinion, 'Micah's connection with Jonah as an adjoining book is not significant, but this sixth book in the Twelve does have a close relationship with its five predecessors as a whole' (House 1990: 85). Davies and Clines (1993: 197) note that there are at least thirteen shared catchwords between the end of Micah (7.8-20) and the beginning of Nahum (ch. 1). There are nouns and verbs, common (such as 'river') and less common such as the names 'Bashan' and 'Carmel', in the same context. Micah 1.3-4 and Nah. 1.3-5 have similarities between them in terms of God having a cosmic effect on the world.

Dempster is one of the few, it seems, who wrestles with Micah's place in MT between Jonah and Nahum. He observes that Jonah is saved by the LORD from the depths of the waters (Jon. 2.10) and in Micah, the LORD saves the people by 'hurling their sins down to the depths of the water (Mic. 7:19)' (Dempster 2017: 55). The nations are threatened with punishment if they do not obey in Micah (5.15) and in Nahum, that judgement is announced because of their wickedness (Dempster 2017: 55). He proposes (2017: 55): 'That Micah, which is addressed to Israel and Judah, is sandwiched between two books dealing with the city of Nineveh shows that God's mercy does not come at the expense of his justice.' Jonah and Nahum both end with questions about justice and mercy. Dempster views Nahum as demonstrating that God will end her endless cruelty.

> The unique position of Micah between these two books dealing with the nations shows the importance of the remnant for its ministry to the nations. In the salvation of the remnant lies the salvation of the world. When the remnant is brought back to Jerusalem and its final king comes to Zion to reform it, it will be exalted to the highest place and become a beacon to the nations. The nations that come and change will be saved – this is the message of Jonah (Mic 4:1–5). Those who do not will be judged – this is the message of Nahum (Mic 5:15). (Dempster 2017: 55–6)

Indeed, justice, judgement and mercy are key themes that run across the three books and while justice is a prominent theme in most of the OT, the polarization of it in Jonah and Nahum emphasizes it. In short and to simplify it, there is no punishment on the Ninevites from God in Jonah and not much other than his punishment in Nahum. As Feinberg (1951: 154) says, the LORD is revealed immediately as a/the Judge in Micah with the nations being called as witnesses to God's bearing witness against Samaria (Israel) and Jerusalem (Judah) which brings the book of Micah straight into the question of God's justice. Unlike Jonah and Nahum, though, God's judgement in Micah is complex, with doom and hope intertwined. Also, as Mic. 2.7 makes clear, the same words have different effects depending on who the listener is: 'Do not My words do good / To the one walking uprightly?' Jonah and Nahum are, in effect, two views of the same situation, but in Jonah the Ninevites decide to walk uprightly whereas in Nahum they do not. It is not simply a matter of 'this is what life looks like if you repent (Jonah) and this is what life looks like if you do not (Nahum)', however, and Micah – sandwiched between them – brings another perspective.

Micah's positioning between Jonah and Nahum in the MT has at least two possible theological interpretative functions. The first is that Micah demonstrates that judgement and justice are more nuanced than they appear in either of the other two books. The prophet Jonah does not like total mercy and forgiveness, perhaps because it is 'unjust' because the Ninevites see no consequences to their actions. The book of Nahum does not need a character who dislikes its contents: centuries of Jews and Christians have managed that by themselves. I suggested in my chapter on Nahum that Jonah and Nahum may be used in contemporary communities of faith to think about retribution, vengeance, justice and judgement. What do traumatized people who have suffered brutally at the hands of oppressors want in terms of God's judgement on their enemies? Micah is helpful in providing a more complex view – the context is far larger than Nineveh and Assyria, there is lament and wailing over judgement (Mic. 1.8-9), God refuses to listen to the cries of the wicked leaders (3.4) but pardons iniquity and has compassion (7.18-19), when God judges between nations there is an end to war (4.1-5), there are evil rulers (3.1-4) but also a good one from a lowly clan (5.2), and there is a powerful remnant (5.7-8) among other things. Micah is not, after all, the middle ground between Jonah and Nahum as if there was a linear scale of punishment from nothing to everything. Good thinking about judgement, retribution, justice, vengeance and punishment requires people to engage with God, humanity and even creation and the cosmos, and there is a chance that if there is a right answer, then it might not be within the grasp of those crying for God's unchecked judgement on their enemies or those praying for indiscriminate mercy and forgiveness. There are various avenues down which one might take the discussion further, but this is not the place, suffice to say that an end result might push the faithful back to the Torah to Gen. 18.25, 'Shall not the Judge of all the earth deal justly?' and also, for Christians, forward to the Cross and the Resurrection.

The second interpretative move for understanding Micah's place between Jonah and Nahum is related to the above point. The book of Micah is probably best known today for its call to social justice, particularly 6.8, 'He has told you, O man [mortal], what is good; / And what does the LORD require of you / But to do justice, to love kindness, / And to walk humbly with your God?' Micah 3.1-2 addresses the leaders by asking, 'Is it not for you to know justice? / You who hate good and love evil'. This first line, 'Is it not for you to know justice?' is a double entendre, an ambiguity that is in both the Hebrew and the Greek. In fact, there are three ways of understanding this rhetorical question that carries the implicit answer 'yes': (1) the leaders should know justice in terms of understanding what it is; (2) but also therefore, know it for themselves experientially in terms of practising it instead of practising injustice, for the verb 'know' often carries with it an intimate knowledge, as is commonly known when people joke about Adam 'knowing' Eve (see also Ogden 2023: 22); and (3) given that they hate good and love evil, it is about time that they knew God's justice upon them in terms of experiencing it (see also Waltke 1993: 657; Ralph Smith 1984: 31; Gignilliat 2019: 131). However one takes the phrase, it is clear that the leaders should know justice. Most, if not all, humans have some sense of justice, let alone leaders of God's people. Micah's challenge to the leaders (and to all who read the book as Scripture) is to practise justice. Jonah and Nahum are primarily concerned with God's justice, as is Micah, but what Micah brings out clearly (though the idea is present in Nahum and to a lesser extent in Jonah as well) is that humans are to be just. Justice does not only belong to God's realm. In that sense, Micah pulls the attention away somewhat from human thinking about what it means for God to be just, to focus more on what humans should be doing to be just themselves.

The book of Jonah finishes with God's question to Jonah about having compassion on Nineveh and then the book of Micah begins with the prophet's name in the first verse; an oblique reference to 'Who is like YHWH?' Micah ends with a few verses explicitly asking who is like God in terms of forgiving iniquities and showing mercy and then comes Nahum with a jealous and avenging God. Who is like God? These three books alone show that the answer is not a straightforward one.

Other theological purposes and themes

'"Justice" was the key theme of Micah's preaching' (Williamson 2013: 598) and is arguably the main motif in the book as a whole. As stated above, justice includes both God's justice and also a requirement for human justice. Kessler (2021: 463) acknowledges that while Micah contains both judgement and salvation, so do most of the prophetic books of the Bible. In Micah, however, there is a stark swapping between the two, plus Micah's particular interest in 'social justice'. Alfaro (1989) writes his Micah commentary from the perspective of a liberation theologian.

There are a number of other theological purposes and themes across Micah. Phillips (2022: 178–81) sees the covenant as a theological emphasis in Micah, with a focus on the covenantal Name, covenant disputes and covenant infidelity with its consequences. She and others point to the remnant theology in Micah, particularly in 2.12 and 4.7. God's forgiveness is another theme in Micah. Micah's name, 'Who is like YHWH?' is considered a theme primarily because of the inclusio nature of the question in 7.18, 'Who is a God like you?' The 'day of the LORD' is a theological motif in Micah, as it is across the book of the Twelve in general. Micah frequently addresses both Israel and Judah, which is a motif in Micah, though not exclusive to the book.

While the book of Micah does not have oracles specifically concerning the nations, the nations are present from the start and throughout. While the word of the LORD which Micah 'saw' primarily concerns Samaria and Jerusalem (Mic. 1.1), the scope is immediately that of the earth and all who live in it (v. 2), which indicates that the LORD's jurisdiction extends beyond Samaria and Jerusalem (see also Dempster 2017: 69). The behaviour of the nations determines their outcome (5.15, 7.13, 16–17) as it does for Israel and Judah. As well, on the Day of the LORD, the nations are included in the new reality of the abolishment of war and in going up to the mountain of the LORD to learn his ways (4.1-5).

When looking at the theological purpose of any book in Scripture, a good question to ask is, 'What does this tell me about God?' Dempster (2017: 2) gives his thoughts on this question:

Throughout the collection of Micah's speeches the audience of Micah, whether ancient or modern, learns a great deal about this God. He is a God who takes his covenant with his people seriously (1:5), who will brook no rivals to transcendence (1:6–7), and who controls the nations—even the dreaded Assyrian army (1:6–16). Yet he is concerned with the plight of the 'little people' and their exploitation at the hands of the covetous rich (2:1–3, 8–9; 3:1–3), with telling the truth (2:6–11; 3:5–8), with a just society and the importance of human rights (6:6–8), with the terrible blight of war in the world (4:1–5), and with what it means to be human (6:6–8). In addition, this God is not a dispassionate, distant figure but one who suffers the pain of the victims, is furious with their oppressors (an implication of the many judgement speeches and also 7:18b), and is exasperated with his people because of their failure to respond to his grace (6:3). This is surely a god like no other, a transcendent one – 'high and lofty' (this is Isaiah's way of describing transcendence in Isa 6:1), but also concerned with matters of mundane reality like fairness and equity, poverty and wealth, widows and orphans.

This might be a good summary of OT prophecy, even the OT in general. Indeed, many key messages are repeated in various forms via different writers in the OT. Neither is Micah's witness of God constrained by this paragraph, and other scholars – even Dempster himself, of course, unrestrained by word count, or in another context – may choose alternative themes to highlight.

Micah in the contemporary world

Reasons for lament (Mic. 1.8-11)

Elaine Phillips (2022: 185) gives six possible war contexts for what caused Micah's initial lament in the first chapter of Micah: (1) Tiglath-Pileser III's sweep through the Shephelah and the Negev in 734 BCE; (2) a Syro-Ephraimite attack on Judah (734–732 BCE) that might have spilled over to the south; (3) Philistine raids; (4) right before or after the fall of Samaria in 722 when Assyrian hostility would have affected the south; (5) Assyrian attacks on Ashdod, accompanied by guerilla raids into the Shephelah (720–712 BCE); or (6) Sennacherib's attacks in 701 BCE. Alternatively, she suggests that the lament might be a result of Tiglath-Pileser III's aggressive moves, rather than war itself.

Micah's lament in the text follows the proclamation of God's judgement (Mic. 1.2-7). Micah's response may be quite different to Jonah's, but their situations are not comparable. Micah laments at least in part if not wholly for his own people and origins: Judah and Israel. Jonah's message was to a cruel enemy. In his section on interpreting Micah's word now, Dempster (2017: 79) writes: 'Micah's lamentation is a type of Jesus's lamentation over Jerusalem (Mt. 23:37), and surely such grief should melt the hard hearts of believers and unbelievers alike, and induce them to wake up.' If Jonah-Micah-Nahum encourage thinking about issues of justice, punishment and vengeance, then Micah's response of lament is one worth considering, even if it is ultimately rejected.

Punishment-town wordplays (Mic. 1.10-16)

Dempster (2017) describes the wordplay in 1.10-16 as 'overkill' because the sounds and meanings of the place names are wordplays on their ensuing punishment: 'their names seal their fate' (41). While contemporary Westerners see wordplays and puns as 'clever and witty' (Dempster 2017: 41), the ancient Hebrews would not have done, but would have seen them as 'significant – even ominous' (41). On page 66 of his commentary, he gives a helpful table with the place name, the transliteration of the Hebrew, the English translation and then his own version which brings out the wordplays: In Tell Town [Gath] don't tell it; in Dust House [Beth-leaphrah] roll in the dust; get yourselves out of there in nakedness and shame, residents of Beauty Town [Shaphir]; no exit for Exit Town [Zaanan]; the mourning of Neighbour Town [Beth-ezel] means no more neighbour; for the residents of Bitterville [Maroth] hoped for better; for war has come down from the LORD to the gate of the City of Peace [Jerusalem]; bind the chariot to the harness, residents of Harness Town [Lachish]; therefore you will give parting gifts to Inheritance of Gath [Moresheth-Gath]; the houses of deception [Achzib] will prove deceptive to the kings of Israel; I will bring a conqueror to Conquering Town [Mareshah]; and, unto the land of the caves [Adullam] will flee the glory of Israel.

Land grabbing and identity (Mic. 2.1-2)

Alfaro (1989: 22–3) notes that the Israelite's covenant ensured that land stayed within families and suggests that:

> landgrabbing came to be considered the worst of threats to the socioreligious system based on the Covenant traditions of Exodus. Landgrabbing became

a serious problem in the history of Israel and Judah, as attested by the denunciations we find in Scripture (cf. Isa. 5:8–9; Deut. 27:17; Prov. 23:10–11; Neh. 5:1–3; 1 Sam. 8:11, 14–17; 1 Kgs 21:1–23). Isaiah and Micah make landgrabbing the first target in a series of various denunciations: Deut. 27:17 puts it at the head of a list of sins against property, after the sins against God and one's own family. Landgrabbing was a capital sin, the root of many other sins and injustices. (1989: 23)

Other commentators have commented similarly, if not always as strongly (e.g. Mays 1976: 63–4; Ralph Smith 1984: 24; Limburg 1988: 170; Waltke 1993: 635; Simundson 1996: 549–50, 551).

Coomber (2021: 208–23) explains that as subsistence societies are absorbed into centralized systems, administrative elites often introduce debt schemes in order to satisfy the desires of the administrators, even if they are not the needs of the producers. For instance, producers are pressurised into taking high-risk ventures that might lead to a higher yield or more specialized crops but are also more liable to fail. Coomber asserts that the administrators are cynical in their approach and intend the farmers to fail so that they can incorporate small family plots into their large, corporate one. Thus, the administrators become rich at the expense of rural producers who suffer exploitation and displacement. This is not a new phenomenon as can be seen from Mic. 2.1-2: 'Alas for those who devise wickedness and evil deeds on their beds! When the morning dawns, they perform it, because it is in their power. They covet fields, and seize them; houses, and take them away; they oppress householder and house, people and their inheritance.' He also comments that this was also the situation at the time when he considers that the book of Micah was being written in the Persian period. As is so often the case with the Old Testament, the perpetrators of the evil deeds are not identified and while scholars have proposed various possibilities, the text is open to anyone abusing power and economically oppressing, even impoverishing, the everyday worker.

Joseph Lalfakzuala (2019: 148–64) has a different perspective, however. He argues that scholars have often drawn on social science and made their conclusions about land ownership abuse from that. Drawing on a Northeast Indian tribal experience, he claims that in Mic. 2.1–2, people do not only lose their land, but their identity. That is, a tribal people's identity is linked to the land, and he gives the example that when asked when they were born, a person from a Northeast Indian tribe is likely to answer that it was when their parents were tilling such-and-such a field at a certain point in the agricultural calendar. Furthermore, Lalfakzuala argues, the land connects a tribal people to its ancestors as well as the community (152). 'If the land is lost, the clan's identity too will be lost' (152), for the 'land provides not only their economic needs but also sociological and psychological needs of the people. It provides not only a life-support system but also a sense of belonging and spirituality' (153). He concludes that it is not unlikely that Israel only became a nation when she had land and stopped being a nation when she lost it (153). Mays (1976: 63–4) and Jon L. Dybdahl (1981: 128) have a similar view in that the loss of land is the loss of family and societal ties.

Lalfakzuala argues that in Isaiah's and Micah's time, tribal and clan solidarity was weakening. Being driven from the land and the community 'was absolutely devastating for an individual or household in tribal societies. Therefore, the encroachment and seizure of land in Israelite society was not simply a political and economic oppression. It represented a destruction of the socio-cultural fabric, an attack on religious people's freedom and identity, and a violation of a close-knit community's ways of life, customs and traditions' (2019: 159). Prophets such as Micah would likely have witnessed small farmers suffering this fate and thus protested vehemently against it.

Responsibility not reliance (Mic. 3.9-11; 6.8)

In Mic. 3.9-11 (similar to Jer. 7.1-15), the leaders accept bribes and are socially corrupt but presume that they are safe because they have the temple of the LORD. Yisca Zimran (2021:14), as part of a larger argument about Jerusalem's destruction not being an end in itself, contends that Micah requires that the leaders 'lessen their reliance on God' and, instead, 'take true responsibility for their actions themselves within society' (14).

Isaiah and Micah talk together (Mic. 5.9-14 and Isa. 2.6-22)

Zimran proposes a reading strategy whereby the similar units of Mic. 5.9-14 and Isa. 2.6-22 be read as a quasi-dialogue, particularly regarding the definition of idolatry and the reason why Micah objects to it (Zimran 2020: 432). One of the results of doing this is that the emphases of each book become more apparent in the light of the comparison with the other book. For instance, she sees Micah as portraying pride and idolatry as two different realities, whereas Isaiah describes the two together. Zimran thus concludes that Micah's separation of the two is significant, for it shows his attitude to them (Zimran 2020: 432). Another example relates to the Day of the LORD. Micah directs his speech towards Israel while Isaiah directs his to the nations. This may demonstrate, Zimran argues, a variety in biblical positions concerning the matter, or that these issues were debated either at the time of their authorship or redaction – or even at the time of analysis in modern scholarship.

> The details cannot always all be explained precisely, and one cannot always reach a unified conclusion regarding their meaning; however, the differences between the units cannot be ignored and the units cannot be read entirely harmoniously. A comparative reading enables us to note and emphasize the differences, and therefore ascribe the appropriate significance to the details. (433)

God cannot be bribed (Mic. 6.1-8)

Coomber writes that Mic. 6.1-8 makes it clear that divine mercy is not something that can be haggled over with rituals and sacrifices. It is not a matter of making many sacrifices of animals, oil, or even children, in the hopes of appeasing the LORD and turning away his anger (6.6-7). 'YHWH is not a god who shares in their depraved approach to power' (Coomber 2021: 221). This also means that those who cannot offer material gifts are not at a disadvantage. Rather, God requires right behaviour (6.8). This applies to everyone, irrespective of economic status.

Theophanies reworked (Mic. 7.7-20)

The most debated issue with regard to Mic. 7.7-20 is whether v. 7 belongs with the verses that precede it (vv. 1-6) or those that follow it (vv. 8-20), or even if it should be read with both the verses that precede and those that follow it (Banister 2018: 27). With regard to the text, Jamie Banister notes that a number of common storm-/warrior-god theophany motifs are missing in Mic. 7.7-20. That is, there is no description of divine weapons or of God's descent from a holy mountain or temple, there is no mythic battle, and nature is not affected by God's coming. Mic. 1.2-4 is a more traditional theophanic passage (Banister 2018: 41). She nevertheless contends that Mic. 7.7-20 does contain other motifs that are common to theophanies: both the land and humans are affected – land is made desolate (v. 13), humans are humiliated (vv. 10, 16) and nations fear (v. 17); God's anger is portrayed (v. 9) where the word used 'connotes a kind of storming rage that is explicitly connected with theophanic imagery in Isa 30:30' (Banister 2018: 43); and God's character of Saviour (v. 7) is brought out. The same places that appear in other theophanic passages appear here as well, particularly Bashan, Carmel and Gilead (Banister 2018: 41–4). Banister surmises that the earlier storm-/warrior-god motif has been modified to reduce the anthropomorphic language because 'the author of Micah 7 is careful to avoid any implication that YHWH has a physical form despite the use of language common in theophanies' (44–5). She does a cross-analysis of Mic. 7.7-20, Habakkuk 3 and Zech. 9.9-16 (135–46) and concludes that Habakkuk 3 is older and the redactor who added Mic. 7.7 as a bridge to connect vv. 1-6 and 8-20 may have been influenced in their choice of verbs by Habakkuk's theme of keeping watch (137).

Trauma studies and Micah (Mic. 1.6–7; 4.1–5, 9–10; 5.3)

Trauma studies is a relatively new field and Rainer Kessler (2021: 470) gives a very brief overview of those who have read Micah through this lens. Alphonso Groenewald's reading of Mic. 4.1-5 is one such example. The text immediately follows 3.12, a text that 'arouses pictures of chaos and trauma' from the perspective of the readers of the text. Read against the background of 3.12, Mic. 4.1-5 becomes 'an agrarian anti-war protest,' or 'a voice of protest against the trauma caused by the politics of the governing elite of Jerusalem' (Groenewald 2018, 363–4).

Feminist readings and gender studies are no longer new fields, but as Kessler points out, scholars such as Juliana Claasens are combining gender and trauma readings, for example, looking at the woman in labour in Mic. 4.9-10 and Mic. 5.3. Kessler observes that while in 3.10, labour depicts pain and anguish, the focus of 5.3 is the result of labour – the baby – who is one who brings hope (Kessler 2021: 469). Kessler (2021: 469) also notices that while Moses, Aaron and Miriam are mentioned together (Num. 26.59) and Miriam leads the women in dancing after the Exodus (Exod. 15.20-22), Mic. 6.4 is the only text in the Hebrew Bible where Miriam is included along with Moses and Aaron as one of the leaders of the Exodus.

As Kessler (2021: 469) and others point out, Samaria is personified as a woman and compared to a prostitute in Mic. 1.6-7. This imagery, used elsewhere in the OT, is problematic, not least because the abuse of women is so tied up with prostitution. Scholars who are interested in rape and sexual violence in the Old Testament tend not to concentrate on Micah, however. For instance, Pamela Gordon and Harold Washington (1995: 315) simply note that Mic. 4.11 depicts the punishment of Jerusalem as sexual humiliation.

Micah in Africa (Mic. 2.12-13; 3.5; 6.6-8; 7.1-6)

A number of recent papers on Micah have come out from Pretoria University in South Africa which use Micah in specific ways to understand and address African situations. Kasebwe T. Kabongo (2021), for instance, in considering Mic. 6.8, looks at how one Christian organization sought in different ways to practise loving justice in the disruption caused by the Covid-19 restrictions. As well as attending those in need, this also meant raising the status of women to leadership in the organization. Solomon Ademiluka (2022) focuses on Mic. 7.3 where the prince and the judge ask for a bribe, and he compares it to the situation in Nigeria where it is normal for law enforcement agents to require bribes from motorists (though Ademiluka makes the point that this is actually extortion rather than bribery). Blessing Boloje, as part of his research on ethics and socio-economics in Micah, has written a few papers, which include advocating as normative the relational shepherd-king model in Mic. 2.12-13, which is carried out in community, and which involves protecting people from harm (2020); arguing that the food metaphor in Mic. 3.5 is associated with economic exploitation and religious abuse of power – an image that can speak to Africans in a materialistic context (2021b); that ritual and lifestyle go hand in hand (Mic. 6.6–8) (2019); and suggesting (with his eye on corruption in Africa) that the prophet's lament in Mic. 7.1-6, 'indicates that corruption threatens the general well-being and prosperity of society, as it creates a fragmented and disorganized society in which social vices flourish' (2021a: 7).

Conclusion

Micah is a book that perhaps exemplifies more than most, with its position (in the MT) between Jonah and Nahum, the different contextual levels at which a book may be read. On its own, it has much to say about social justice, judgement and salvation. Positioned between Jonah and Nahum, its material on the complexities of justice and mercy stand in stark contrast to those of its neighbouring books. It is also a book that demonstrates how positioning in the canon may affect interpretation, for Micah does not stand between Jonah and Nahum in the LXX. With its abrupt changes in subject (perhaps because of its compositional history), the book of Micah can be choppy reading for the new or infrequent reader. As a number of scholars have shown, however, there is coherence, even consistency in the book. While its historical setting is the time of Assyrian power in the mid- to late-eighth century and into the beginning of the seventh, for many writers, its words are relevant in the contemporary world, whether that world be the West, NE India or Africa.

References

Ademiluka, Solomon (2022), ' "[T]he Prince and the Judge Ask for a Bribe" (Mi 7:3): Interpreting the Old Testament Prophets on Bribery in Light of the Encounter between Motorists and Law Enforcement Agents on Nigerian Highways'. *Verbum et Ecclesia* (online), February.

Alfaro, Juan I. (1989). *Micah: Justice and Loyalty*. Grand Rapids, MI: Eerdmans.

Andersen, F. I., and D. N. Freedman (2000). *Micah: A New Translation with Introduction and Commentary*, Vol. 24E. New Haven, CT: Yale University Press.

Banister, Jamie A. (2018). *The God of Thunder and War in Micah, Habakkuk, and Zephaniah*, Gorgias Biblical Studies 68. Piscataway, NJ: Gorgias Press.

Boloje, Blessing (2019). 'Extravagant Rituals or Ethical Religion (Micah 6:6–8)? Ritual Interface with Social Responsibility in Micah'. *Old Testament Essays* (OTE) 32 (3): 800–20.

Boloje, Blessing (2020). 'Micah's Shepherd-King (Mi 2:12–13): An Ethical Model for Reversing Oppression in Leadership Praxis'. *Verba et Ecclesia* (online), September.

Boloje, Blessing (2021a). ' "The Godly Person Has Perished from the Land" (Mi 7:1–6): Micah's Lamentation of Judah's Corruption and Its Ethical Imperatives for a Healthy Community Living'. *HTS Teologiese Studies/ Theological Studies* (online), August.

Boloje, Blessing (2021b). 'Exploring Religious Power: A Re-reading of Micah's Metaphor of Food (Mi 3:5) in the Context of African Religious Space'. *Verba et Ecclesia* (online), October.

Brueggemann, Walter (1981). '"Vine and Fig Tree": A Case Study in Imagination and Criticism'. *Catholic Biblical Quarterly*, 43 (1981): 188-204.

Coomber, Matthew (2021). 'Poverty and Social Justice in Micah', in Carly L. Crouch (ed.), *The Cambridge Companion to the Hebrew Bible and Ethics*, 208-23. New York: Cambridge University Press.

Cruz, Juan. (2016). '*Who Is Like Yahweh?': A Study of Divine Metaphors in the Book of Micah*. Göttingen, Germany: Vandenhoeck & Ruprecht.

Cuffey, Kenneth Hugh (1987). 'The Coherence of Micah: A Review of the Proposals and a New Interpretation', PhD diss., Drew University, Madison.

Davies, P. R., and D. J. A. Clines, eds (1993). *Among the Prophets: Language, Image, and Structure in the Prophetic Writings*, Vol. 144, Sheffield: JSOT Press.

Dempster, Stephen G. (2017). *Micah*, Grand Rapids, MI: Eerdmans.

Dempsey, Carol J. (2015). 'Harrowing Woes and Comforting Promises in the Book of the Twelve', in Mark J. Boda, Michael H. Floyd and Colin M. Toffelmire (eds), *The Book of the Twelve and the New Form Criticism*, 85-100. Atlanta, GA: SBL Press Atlanta.

Dempsey, Carol J. (2021). 'Metaphor in the Minor Prophets', in Julia M. O'Brien (ed.), *The Oxford Handbook of the Minor Prophets*, 85-100. New York: Oxford University Press.

Dybdah, Jon L. (1981). 'Israelite Village Land Tenure: Settlement to Exile', PhD diss., Fuller Theological Seminary, Pasadena, CA.

Feinberg, Charles L. (1951). *The Minor Prophets*. Chicago: Moody Press.

Floyd, Michael H. (2021). 'Genres and Forms in the Minor Prophets', in Julia M. O'Brien (ed.), *The Oxford Handbook of the Minor Prophets*, 72-84. New York: Oxford University Press.

Gignilliat, Mark S. (2019). *Micah*, ITC. London: T&T Clark.

Glenny, W. Edward (2015). *Micah, A Commentary Based on Micah in Codex Vaticanus*, Septuagint Commentary Series. Leiden: Brill.

Gordon, Pamela, and Harold C. Washington (1995). 'Rape as a Military Metaphor', in Athalya Brenner (ed.), *A Feminist Companion to the Minor Prophets, Vol. 8, A Feminist Companion to the Bible*, 308-25. London: T&T Clark.

Hagstrom, David Gerald (1988). *The Coherence of the Book of Micah. A Literary Analysis*, SBLDS 89. Atlanta, GA: Scholars Press.

Halvorson-Taylor, Martien A. (2021). 'The Exiles of Empires in Prophetic Images of Restoration (and Micah 4:8-5:1 [ET 5:2])', in Pamela Barmash and Mark W. Hamilton (eds), *In the Shadow of Empire: Israel and Judah in the Long Sixth Century BCE*, 97-113. Atlanta, GA: Society of Biblical Literature.

House, Paul R. (1990). *The Unity of the Twelve*, JSOT Supplement Series 97, Bible and Literature Series 27. Sheffield: Almond Press.

Kessler, Rainer (2021). 'Micah', in Julia M. O'Brien (ed.), *The Oxford Handbook of the Minor Prophets*, 461–71. New York: Oxford University Press.

Kabongo, Kasebwe T. (2021). 'Making Sense of the COVID-19 Disruptions in Incarnational Ministry Using Micah 6:8 as an Interpretive Framework', *Verbum et Ecclesia* (online), September.

Lalfakzuala, J. K. (2019). 'Land Ownership Abuse in Micah 2:1–2 and Isaiah 5:8–10: A New Perspective from a Northeast India Tribal Perspective,' *Bangalore Theological Forum* 51 (1): 148–64.

Limburg, James (1988). *Hosea-Micah*, Interpretation. Atlanta, GA: John Knox.

Mays, J. L. (1976). *Micah: A Commentary*. London: SCM Press.

Moore, Anne (2009). *Moving beyond Symbol and Myth: Understanding the Kingship of God of the Hebrew Bible through Metaphor*. Studies in Biblical Literature 99. New York: Peter Lang, 2009.

Ogden, Graham S. (2023). *Nahum, Habakkuk, and Malachi*, Readings, A New Biblical Commentary. Sheffield: Sheffield Phoenix Press, 2023.

Phillips, Elaine (2022). *Obadiah, Jonah & Micah*, Apollos Old Testament Commentary 23. London: Apollos.

Radine, Jason (2021). 'The Dating of Prophetic Books and the Persian-Period "Turn"', in Julia M. O'Brien (ed.), *The Oxford Handbook of the Minor Prophets*, 17–28. New York: Oxford University Press.

Shepherd, Michael B. (2021). 'The Minor Prophets in Early Christianity', in Julia M. O'Brien (ed.), *The Oxford Handbook of the Minor Prophets*, 243–51. New York: Oxford University Press.

Sieges, Anna (2021). 'One Book or Twelve Books?', in Julia M. O'Brien (ed.), *The Oxford Handbook of the Minor Prophets*, 29–38. New York: Oxford University Press.

Simkovich, Malka Z. (2021). 'The Minor Prophets in Early Judaism', in Julia M. O'Brien (ed.), *The Oxford Handbook of the Minor Prophets*, 228–42. New York: Oxford University Press.

Simundson, Daniel J. (1996). 'The Book of Micah', in Leander E. Keck, Thomas G. Long, Bruce C. Birch, Katheryn Pfisterer Darr, William L. Lane, Gail R. O'Day, David L. Petersen, John J. Collins, Jack A. Keller Jr, James Earl Massey, Marrion L. Soards (eds), *Introduction to Apocalyptic Literature, Daniel, the Twelve Prophets*, Vol. 7 of *The New Interpreter's Bible: A Commentary in Twelve Volumes*, 531–98. Nashville, TN: Abingdon Press.

Smith, John Merlin Powis (1911). 'Micah', in John Merlin Powis Smith, William Hayes Ward and Julius A. Bewer (eds), *A Critical and Exegetical Commentary, on Micah, Zephaniah, Nahum, Habakkuk, Obadiah and Joel*, International Critical Commentary on the Holy Scriptures of the Old and New Testaments, 3–156. Edinburgh: T&T Clark.

Smith, Ralph (1984). *Micah-Malachi*, Word Biblical Commentary 32. Nashville, TN: Nelson Reference and Electronic.

Stansell, Gary (1988). *Micah and Isaiah: A Form and Tradition Historical Comparison*, SBL Dissertation Series 85. Atlanta, GA: Scholars Press.

Sweeney, Marvin A. (2021). 'The Minor Prophets and the Book of the Twelve in Late Eighteenth-Century through Early Twenty-First-Century Research', in Julia M. O'Brien (ed.), *The Oxford Handbook of the Minor Prophets*, 267–78. New York: Oxford University Press.

Trotter, James (2015). 'Reading the "Prophetic Lawsuit" Genre in the Persian Period', in Mark J. Boda, Michael H. Floyd and Colin M. Toffelmire (eds), *The Book of the Twelve and the New Form Criticism*, Ancient Near East Monographs no. 10, 63–74. Atlanta, GA: SBL Press.

Van Hecke, Pierre J. P. (2003). 'Living Alone in the Shrubs: Positive Pastoral Metaphors in Micah 7,14'. *Zeitschri für die alttestamentliche Wissenscha*, 115 (3): 362–75.

Waltke, Bruce (1993). 'Micah', in Thomas Edward McComiskey (ed.), *The Minor Prophets: An Exegetical and Expository Commentary*, Vol. 2. Grand Rapids, MI: Baker Books.

Williamson, H. G. M. (2013). 'Micah', in John Barton and John Muddiman (eds), *The Oxford Bible Commentary*, 595–9. Oxford: Oxford University Press.

Zimran, Yisca (2020). 'Micah 5.9–14 (10–15) and Isaiah 2.6–22: Two Distinctive Perceptions of Idolatry'. *Journal for the Study of the Old Testament*, 44 (3): 420–36.

Zimran, Yisca (2021). '"What Does the Lord Require of You": The Attitude towards Zion and the Social Situation in the Book of Micah'. *Scandinavian Journal of the Old Testament*, 35 (1): 1–18.

Scriptural Index

Genesis	
Genesis (general references to the book)	29
Gen. 2.21	17
Gen. 4.16	15
Gen 7	54
Gen. 7.2	30
Gen. 10.11-12	12
Gen. 18.25	85
Gen. 45.20	36
Exodus	
Exodus (general references to the book)	15, 32, 37, 53, 92
Exod. 15.20-22	92
Exod. 20.5	53
Exod. 34.6	15, 32, 53
Exod. 34.7	15, 32, 53
Exod. 34.14	53
Numbers	
Num. 14.18	32, 53
Num 23:19	92
Deuteronomy	
Deuteronomy (general references to the book)	7
Deut. 4.24	53
Deut. 5.9	53
Deut. 5.14	37
Deut. 6.15	53
Deut. 18.9-12	19
Deut. 23.13	60
Deut. 24.1	50
Deut. 27.17	89
Deut. 32	7
Joshua	
Joshua (general references to book)	14
Josh. 24.19	53
Judges	
Judges (general references to book)	14
Judg. 17–18	74
Ruth	
Ruth (general references to the book)	14
1 Samuel	
1 Samuel (general references to the book)	14
1 Sam. 3.1	49
1 Sam. 8:11	89
1 Sam. 8:14–17	89
2 Samuel	
2 Sam. 22	7
1 Kings	
1 Kings (general reference to the book)	53
1 Kgs 8.52	26
1 Kgs 17.5	26
1 Kgs 17.24	4

1 Kgs 19.10	53	Ps. 88.5	7
1 Kgs 19.12	54	Ps. 88.10-12	7
1 Kgs 19.14	53	Ps. 89.19	49
1 Kgs 21:1–23	89	Ps. 103.8	32
		Ps. 137	69
2 Kings		Ps. 137.8	66
2 Kings (general reference to the book)	4	Ps. 137.9	66, 67
		Ps. 139.8-10	22
		Ps. 139.8	7
2 Kgs 6.25	60	Ps. 145.8	32
2 Kgs 8.11-12	66		
2 Kgs 9.25	48	Proverbs	
2 Kgs 14.25	4, 26	Prov. 16.33	17
2 Kgs 18.27	60	Prov. 18.18	17
		Prov. 23:10-11	89
1 Chronicles		Prov. 29	50
1 Chron. 17.15	49	Prov. 29.18	50
2 Chronicles		Isaiah	
2 Chron. 24.27	48	Isaiah (general references to the book or prophet)	46, 48, 49, 50, 55, 63, 77, 79, 87, 89, 90, 91
2 Chron. 32.32	49		
Nehemiah			
Neh. 5:1–3	89		
Neh. 9.17	32, 53	Isa. 1.1	50
		Isa. 2.2-4	77
Esther		Isa. 2.6-22	90
Esther (general references to the book)	14	Isa. 5:8–9	89
		Isa 6:1	87
		Isa. 9.4	55
		Isa. 13–23	48
Job		Isa. 13.1	48
Job (general references to the person)	27	Isa. 14.28	48
		Isa. 15.1	48
Job 20.7	60	Isa. 17.1	48
		Isa. 19.1	48
		Isa. 19.14	63
Psalms		Isa. 19.23–24	27
Psalms (general references to the book)	7, 21	Isa. 21.1	48
		Isa. 21.11	48
Ps. 6.5	7	Isa. 21.13	48
Ps. 16.10	8	Isa 22.1	48
Ps. 30.9	8	Isa. 23.1	5, 48
Ps. 86.15	32, 53	Isa. 30.6	48
Ps. 88.3	7	Isa 30:30	92

Isa. 38.9-20	7
Isa. 49.26	63
Isa. 51.19	63
Isa. 52.7	55
Isa. 63.6	63
Jeremiah	
Jeremiah (general references to the book or prophet)	6, 26, 49, 76
Jer. 7.1-15	90
Jer. 7.31	19
Jer. 13.13	63
Jer. 14.14	49
Jer. 18	65
Jer. 18.1-10	36
Jer. 19.5	19
Jer. 23.16	49
Jer. 23.33	48
Jer. 23.34	48
Jer. 25.27	63
Jer. 26.17-19	76
Jer. 26.18	76
Jer. 32.35	19
Jer. 36	26
Jer. 36.11	78
Jer. 36.13	78
Jer. 36.28	26
Jer. 48.26	63
Jer. 50	63
Jer. 50.7	63
Jer. 50.15	63
Jer. 50.17-18	63
Jer. 50.29	63
Jer. 50.33-34	63
Jer. 51.24-25	63
Lamentations	
Lam. 2.9	50
Ezekiel	
Ezekiel (general references to the book or prophet)	49, 50
Ezek. 4.12	60
Ezek. 7.13	49
Ezek. 7.26	50
Ezek. 12.10	48
Ezek. 12.24	49
Ezek. 12.27	49
Ezek. 13.16	49
Ezek. 16.20-21	19
Ezek. 23.33	63
Ezek. 23.37	19
Ezek. 25–32	48
Daniel	
Daniel (general references to the book or person)	49
Dan. 1.17	49
Hosea	
Hosea (general references to the book or prophet)	79–83
Hos. 10.14	66
Hos. 12.10	49
Hos. 13.16	66
Joel	
Joel (general references to the book or prophet)	6, 48, 79, 82
Joel 2.13	32, 53
Amos	
Amos (general references to the book or prophet)	4, 27, 48, 50, 75, 79, 81, 82
Obadiah	
Obadiah (general reference to the book or prophet)	14, 48, 50, 67, 79, 82

Scriptural Index

Jonah		Jon. 4	31–7
Jonah (general references to the book or prophet)	1, 3–39, 43, 44, 45, 48, 53, 65, 69, 70, 73, 74, 82–85, 87, 88, 93, 94	Jon. 4.1	10, 31
		Jon. 4.2	10, 15, 31, 32, 35, 37
		Jon. 4.3	33, 34, 35
		Jon. 4.4	33
		Jon. 4.5	33
Jon. 1	6, 12, 13, 14–20, 25, 26, 32	Jon. 4.6	10
		Jon. 4.7	35
Jon. 1.1	13, 14, 53, 83	Jon. 4.8	35
Jon. 1.2	10, 14, 17, 26, 36	Jon. 4.9	34, 35
Jon. 1.3	5, 10, 14, 15, 17	Jon. 4.10	35, 36
Jon. 1.4	10, 16, 19, 31	Jon. 4.11	10, 36, 69, 85
Jon. 1.5	16, 18, 19		
Jon. 1.6	17, 26, 32, 35	Micah	
Jon. 1.7	10	Micah (general references to the book or prophet)	1, 44, 50, 70, 73–94
Jon. 1.8	10		
Jon. 1.9	17, 18, 32		
Jon. 1.10	10, 17, 19		
Jon. 1.12	6, 10, 18, 19	Mic. 1	75, 76, 78, 80, 81, 87
Jon. 1.14	17, 26, 35		
Jon. 1.15	19	Mic. 1–4	75
Jon. 1.16	10, 19	Mic. 1–3	76
Jon. 1.17	10, 20	Mic. 1.1	73, 75, 76, 85
Jon. 2	6, 7, 8, 13, 20–5, 32, 34	Mic. 1.2-3.12	80
		Mic. 1.2–2.13	80
Jon. 2.2	7, 21, 22	Mic. 1.2-7	87
Jon. 2.3	6, 7, 17, 21, 26	Mic. 1.2-4	91
Jon. 2.4	22, 24	Mic. 1.2	86
Jon. 2.6	8, 21, 22	Mic. 1.5	75, 78, 87
Jon. 2.7	24	Mic. 1.6-16	87
Jon. 2.8	24, 39	Mic. 1.6	75, 78, 87, 92
Jon. 2.9	24, 25, 39	Mic. 1.7	87, 92
Jon. 2.10	25	Mic. 1.8-11	87
Jon. 3	6, 12, 22, 26–31, 37	Mic. 1.8-9	84
Jon. 3.1	12	Mic. 1.10-16	88
Jon. 3.2	10, 26, 27	Mic. 1.14	75
Jon. 3.3	10, 11, 27	Mic. 2	75, 76, 80, 81
Jon. 3.4	27, 28	Mic. 2.1-3	87
Jon. 3.5	10, 27, 36	Mic. 2.1–2	88, 89
Jon. 3.6	17, 27, 30	Mic. 2.6-11	87
Jon. 3.7	10, 27, 30	Mic. 2.7	84
Jon. 3.8	5, 10, 17, 30	Mic. 2.8-9	87
Jon. 3.9	31, 35	Mic. 2.12-13	81, 93
Jon. 3.10	10, 31	Mic. 2.12	86

Scriptural Index

Mic. 3.1–4.8	80	Mic. 7.9	92
Mic. 3	75, 76, 80, 81	Mic. 7.10	92
Mic. 3.1-4	84	Mic. 7.13	86, 91
Mic. 3.1-3	87	Mic. 7.14	78
Mic. 3.1-2	85	Mic. 7.16	86, 92
Mic. 3.4	84	Mic. 7.17	86, 92
Mic. 3.5-8	87	Mic. 7.18	78, 84, 86, 87
Mic. 3.5	93	Mic. 7.19	84
Mic. 3.9-11	90	Mic. 7.20	80, 85
Mic. 3.10	92		
Mic. 3.12	76, 80, 81, 92	Nahum	
Mic. 4–7	76	Nahum (general references to the book or prophet)	1, 43–70, 73, 74, 75, 82, 83-5, 88, 93, 94
Mic. 4.1–5.15	80		
Mic. 4	75, 76, 80		
Mic. 4.1-5	83, 86, 87, 92		
Mic. 4.1-4	76		
Mic. 4.1	75, 81	Nah. 1.2–2.3	47
Mic. 4.6	81	Nah. 1	46, 52–5, 65–6, 83
Mic. 4.7	81, 86		
Mic. 4.8–5.2	77	Nah. 1.1	44
Mic. 4.9–5.15	80	Nah. 1.2	52, 53, 55
Mic. 4.9–10	92	Nah. 1.3-5	83
Mic. 4.11	93	Nah. 1.3	32, 52, 53
Mic. 5	76, 80	Nah. 1.4	52, 54
Mic. 5.2	81, 84	Nah. 1.6	54
Mic. 5.3	92	Nah. 1.7	47, 52, 54
Mic. 5.7	84	Nah. 1.8	47, 52, 54
Mic. 5.8	84	Nah. 1.9	54
Mic. 5.14	80	Nah. 1.10	54, 88
Mic. 5:15	80, 83, 86, 88	Nah. 1.11	54, 55
Mic. 6.1–7.20	80	Nah. 1.12	45, 54, 55
Mic. 6	75, 80	Nah. 1.13	45, 54, 55
Mic. 6.1-8	91	Nah. 1.14	54, 55
Mic. 6.3	87	Nah. 1.15	44, 54, 55
Mic. 6.6	87, 91, 93	Nah. 2	52, 55-6
Mic. 6.7	87, 91, 93	Nah 2.1	44, 65
Mic. 6.8	85, 87, 90, 91, 93	Nah. 2.2-13	56
		Nah. 2.2	65
Mic. 6.9-15	81	Nah. 2.3	44, 65
Mic. 7	75, 80, 92	Nah. 2.4	65
Mic. 7.1-6	91, 92, 93	Nah. 2.5	55, 56
Mic. 7.3	93	Nah. 2.6	55, 58
Mic. 7.7-20	91, 92	Nah. 2.7	56, 58, 66
Mic. 7.7	91, 92	Nah. 2.8	52, 55, 56
Mic. 7.8-20	83, 91, 92	Nah. 2.9	44, 56

Scriptural Index

Nah. 2.10	56	Zephaniah	
Nah. 2.11	56	Zephaniah (general	
Nah. 2.12	56, 58	references to	
Nah. 2.13	56	the book)	48, 78, 79, 82
Nah. 3	51, 56, 57–64		
Nah. 3.1-4	44	Zechariah	
Nah. 3.1-3	57	Zechariah (general	
Nah. 3.1	61	references to the book)	48, 82
Nah. 3.4	52, 57, 59, 61	Zech. 9.1	48
Nah. 3.5	57, 58, 59	Zech. 9.9-16	92
Nah. 3.6	52, 59, 60, 61, 62	Zech. 12.1	48
Nah. 3.7	44, 59, 61, 63	Malachi	
Nah. 3.8	45, 52, 61, 62	Malachi (general	
Nah. 3.9	61, 62	references to the	
Nah. 3.10	61, 62, 66	book or prophet)	48, 82
Nah. 3.11	63		
Nah. 3.12	63	Matthew	
Nah. 3.13	58, 63	Mt. 2.5	81
Nah. 3.14	52, 63	Mt. 12.39	4
Nah. 3.15	52, 63	Mt. 12.40	23
Nah. 3.16	52, 63, 64	Mt. 23.37	88
Nah. 3.17	52, 63, 64		
Nah. 3.18	44, 64	Luke	
Nah. 3.19	61, 64, 69	Luke 15	33
Habakkuk		John	
Habakkuk (general		John 11	23
references to the			
book or prophet)	48, 50, 82, 92	1 Timothy	
Hab. 3	92	1 Tim. 3.16-17	68

Subject Index

acrostic 46, 47, 50
Africa 5, 93, 94
agricultural 74, 89
Amittai 4, 14, 25
anger 31–35, 51, 53, 79, 91, 92
animals 3, 8, 10, 11, 16, 30, 31, 37, 39, 91
Assyria 3–6, 12, 27, 33, 44–46, 51, 55, 56, 59, 61, 64, 67, 74, 75, 77, 84, 87, 94
avenge – *see* 'vengeance'

Babylon 44, 45, 48, 59, 63, 66, 77
belly – *see also* 'womb' 7, 21–25, 28
boat – *see* 'ship'
breakers 21, 22
bribe 90, 91, 93

call 14, 17–19, 22, 26, 30
Canonical positioning 1, 14, 70, 73, 75, 82–83, 93, 94
city 37, 45, 58, 68, 75, 79, 88
  of Nineveh – *see* 'Nineveh'
comfort 44, 53, 61, 63, 67, 77
community 46, 78, 90, 93
compassion 22, 26, 36–38, 44, 53, 69, 84, 85
covenant 53, 86–88
cruelty 37, 66
  of Nineveh 5, 44–46, 57, 61, 64–65, 67, 83, 88

dating 4–6, 45, 46, 76, 77
day(s) 49, 73, 76
  Day of the Lord 86, 91
  for 'three days' – *see* 'three'
dead/death 7, 15, 17, 23, 51
  Jonah's 15, 19, 23, 25, 33, 35

Ninevites' 57, 61, 66
  place of dead/death – *see also* 'Sheol' 7, 8, 23
deliverance 7, 21, 25, 33, 35
destruction 53, 54, 66, 74, 75, 90
  God's destructive power 35, 53, 63, 77
  Nineveh's 26, 33, 56, 61
  Nineveh as destroyer 33, 59
down – *see also* 'up' 14–17, 21, 22, 83

Egypt 27, 48, 61, 74
Elkosh 43, 48, 75
evil – *see also* 'wicked' 6, 10, 11, 84, 85, 89
  Nineveh's (in the book of Jonah) 10, 30, 31, 36, 37
  Nineveh's (in the book of Nahum) 53, 59, 61, 67, 69
exaggeration 9–12, 34, 37, 64

farmers 74, 89, 90
fasting 3, 10, 11, 29, 30, 34
fear 16, 51, 56, 92
  Jonah's 3, 17, 18, 19, 21, 22
  the sailor's (in the Book of Jonah) 3, 10, 18, 19
female 14, 23–25, 58
fiction 8, 9
filth 60, 62
final form 1, 76, 78, 81
fish (in the book of Jonah) 3, 5–7, 9, 11, 12, 17, 20–25, 28, 34, 35, 37
foreign (Gentile nations and their people) 4, 14, 17, 24–25, 27–29, 33–34, 37, 48, 53, 64
forgiveness 13, 85, 86
  God's, of Nineveh 5, 15, 32, 33, 38, 84

Subject Index

Gath – *see also* 'Moresheth-Gath' 75, 88
genre 9
    of Jonah 6–9, 13
    of Micah 79–80
    of Nahum 48–51, 57
geographical 4, 5, 8, 43, 73, 75
gourd – *see* 'plant'
grandiose – *see* 'exaggeration'
grace (God's) 22, 32, 36, 38, 53, 69, 80, 87
grave – *see* 'Sheol'
great 6, 10, 29, 31, 34, 53, 54
    city (Nineveh – in Jonah) 12, 14, 26–27, 36
    fear – *see also* 'fear' 10, 18, 19
    fish (in Jonah) 3, 9, 11, 20, 25, 35, 37
    men (in Nahum) 62, 66
    wind/storm (in Jonah) 16, 18, 19, 25

historical 51
    setting of Jonah 4–5, 8, 9, 30
    setting of Micah 73–75, 76–77, 80, 94
    setting of Nahum 44–47, 50
humour 3, 9–11, 37, 38
hurl 6, 16, 18, 19, 83

idol 24, 55, 60, 74, 90
injustice 74, 85, 89
irony
    in Jonah 19, 24, 31, 36, 38
        in/of Jonah's speech 15, 17, 33, 35
    in Nahum 55, 64

jealous 52, 53, 86
Jerusalem 5, 43, 63, 74, 75, 78, 79, 82–84, 86, 88, 90, 92, 93
Jesus 4, 9, 23, 88
judge 38, 79, 85, 93
judgement 63, 79, 80, 94
    against foreign nations 58, 65, 82–84, 86, 87
    against God's people 55, 58, 82, 84, 86, 87
justice 68, 88
    of God 33, 38, 83–86, 94
    of humans 70, 74, 79, 85–87, 89, 93–94

king 33, 45, 78, 83
    of Assyria 44, 55, 64
    of Nineveh 6, 10–12, 29–33, 35

lament 7, 81, 84, 87, 88, 93
larger-than-life – *see* 'exaggeration'
lion 52, 56, 58, 64
location – *see* 'geographical'
locust 52, 63, 64
lots 17, 62
LXX 29, 47, 57, 60, 70, 78, 82, 94

male 14, 23–25, 55, 58, 62
mercy 38, 83–84, 94
    of God 5, 30, 32, 33, 53, 84, 91
    of humans 30, 33
metaphor
    in Jonah 5, 8, 10, 21, 22
    in Micah 78, 93
    in Nahum 51, 52, 54, 56–58, 60, 62, 63
midrash 8, 23, 74
Moresheth-Gath 75, 88

Neo-Assyria – *see* 'Assyria' 64, 74
Nineveh 1, 3–6, 10–12, 14, 15, 17, 18, 20, 23, 24, 26–34, 36, 37, 43–46, 48, 51–61, 63–69, 83–85
Ninevites 15, 17, 25, 29–33, 35–37, 53, 56, 64–66, 84
No-amon 45, 46, 61–63

oppression 65, 67–69, 74, 84, 87, 89, 90
    Nineveh's (as oppressor) 33, 59
Owen, Wilfred 65, 66

perish 31, 33, 35, 37
plant 3, 12, 13, 31, 34–36
poet / poetry 8, 51, 52, 56, 57, 65, 66, 80
prayer 17, 61, 67
    Jonah's 6, 7, 21–25, 32
    sailors' (in Jonah) 16, 19, 20, 35
prostitute 52, 57–60, 62, 92, 93
psalm 6–8, 12, 20, 21, 25, 32

Subject Index

rabbinic 13, 23, 74
rape 57, 58, 93
redaction 1, 11, 46, 47, 76, 77, 91, 92
remnant 83, 84, 86
repentance 15, 21, 23, 24, 49, 79, 84
    Ninevites' 11, 12, 26, 29–34, 36–37, 65
restoration 52, 55, 77, 79, 80
reversal 3, 27, 32, 36, 57, 68, 79
rhetoric 13, 36, 46, 51, 54, 61, 69
rise – *see also* 'up' 14, 15, 18, 22, 26
river 21, 54, 55, 83

sacrifice 18–20, 24, 25, 34, 91
sailors (in Jonah) 3, 16–22, 24, 25, 27, 31–33, 35
salvation 18, 21, 33, 56
   in Micah 74, 79, 83, 86, 92, 94
   Jonah's 16, 20, 22, 25, 32, 83
Samaria 4, 75, 78, 82, 84, 86, 87, 92
sea 7, 11, 44, 48, 54, 74
   in Jonah 5, 16–19, 21–22, 25
Septuagint – *see* LXX
shame 28, 57–60, 70, 88
shelter (in Jonah) 33–35
Sheol 7, 16, 21–24, 55
ship (in Jonah) 5, 15–18, 19, 22, 27, 33, 35
sleep 16, 17, 22
sovereignty 32, 68
stars 63, 64
storm 52, 54, 91, 92
   in Jonah 3, 12, 16–19, 25
structure 6, 12–13, 53, 78, 80–81, 83
suffering 38, 56, 57, 62, 66–69, 84, 87, 89, 90
   under Nineveh / Assyria 33, 44, 61, 67
sun 21, 31, 33–35, 64
superscription 13, 14, 76

Tarshish 5, 14, 15, 24, 32
temple 5, 24, 25, 78, 90, 91

thanksgiving 7, 8, 20, 25, 34
Thebes – *see* No-amon
theology/theological
   in Jonah 6, 8, 18, 23, 25, 27, 32, 34, 38
   in Micah 75, 84, 86
   in Nahum 52, 64, 68–69
theophany 54, 79, 91, 92
three 23, 29
   days (and nights) 11, 12, 22, 23, 29
throw – *see* 'hurl'
trauma 84, 92
twelve 48, 75, 81–83, 86

underworld – *see* Sheol
up – *see also* 'down' and 'rise' 13–15, 18, 22, 25, 86

vengeance 19, 44, 56, 66–67, 84, 88
   of God 52, 53, 55–57, 59–61, 66–67, 69, 86
violence 29, 52, 58, 66, 79, 93
   Nineveh's 5, 30
vision 43, 48–53, 57, 59, 65, 66, 70, 80
vows 20, 24, 25

war 45, 59, 63, 65–67, 69, 87–88
   anti-war 56, 62, 65–68, 92
   end to 84, 86
waves – *see* 'breakers'
wicked – *see also* 'evil' 6, 10, 11, 33, 49, 55, 84, 89
   Nineveh 3, 5, 14, 26, 27, 36, 83
wind 3, 16, 18, 19, 31, 52, 54
womb – *see also* 'belly' 21, 23, 25
word(s), God's 14, 18, 25, 26, 84, 86
wordplay 11, 16, 44, 88
worm 3, 12, 31, 34–36
worship 15, 19, 24, 28, 53, 59

Zion 75, 76, 79, 82, 83